THE PARADOXES

OF LOVE

LLEWELLYN VAUGHAN-LEE

First published in the United States in 1996 by
The Golden Sufi Center
P.O. Box 428, Inverness, California 94937

© 1996 by The Golden Sufi Center

Cover Illustration by Tennessee Dixon.
Printed and bound by Thomson-Shore, Inc.
using recycled paper.

Library of Congress Cataloging in Publication Data,
Vaughan-Lee, Llewellyn
The Paradoxes of Love:
1. Spiritual life
2. Dreams—Religious aspects
3. Sufism

Library of Congress Catalog Card Number: 96-075080
ISBN 0-9634574-6-2

CONTENTS

PREFACE

Throughout this book, in an effort to maintain continu-
ity and simplicity of text, God, the Great Beloved, is
referred to as He. Of course, the Absolute Truth is
neither masculine nor feminine. As much as It has a
divine masculine side, so It has an awe-inspiring
feminine aspect.

~

Abû Saʿîd al-Kharrâz was asked,
"Through what have you known Allâh?"
He replied, "Through the fact that He brings opposites together,"
for he had witnessed their coming together in himself.

~

THE PARADOXES OF LOVE

The storming of love is what is sweetest within her,
Her deepest abyss is her most beautiful form,
To lose our way in her is to arrive,
To hunger for her is to feed and to taste,
Her despairing is sureness of faith,
Her worst wounding is to become whole again,
To waste away for her is to endure,
Her hiding is to find her at all times,
To be tormented for her is to be in good health,
In her concealment she is revealed,
What she withholds, she gives,
Her finest speech is without words,
Her imprisonment is freedom,
Her most painful blow is her sweetest consolation,
Her giving is her taking away,
Her going away is her coming near,
Her deepest silence is her highest song,
Her greatest wrath is her warmest thanks,
Her greatest threatening is remaining true,
Her sadness is the healing of all sorrow.

Hadewijch of Brabant, a 13th Century Beguine[1]

INTRODUCTION

In every moment this love is more endless,
in every time people are more bewildered in it.

'Attâr

Love is the greatest power in the universe. Love is the
dynamic center of life, the energy that is at the very
core of creation. The mystic uses the energy of love to
make the greatest of journeys: the journey of the soul
back to the source, the lover back into the arms of the
Beloved. The power of love transforms the seeker,
revealing within the heart the secrets of oneness, the
mystical truth that lies behind the veils of duality: "All
is One." For the Sufi this truth is stamped in the
shahâda, the protestation "*Lâ ilâha illâ llâh*" (There is
no god but God). The lover recognizes only the face of
the Beloved, realizing that duality is an illusion and
only He exists.

The journey from multiplicity back to oneness, the
"journey back to God," is an unfolding of the heart's
secret. But while the heart knows the reality of His
oneness, the mind and the ego are caught in duality
and the illusion of separation. The heart knows that
only He exists and we are just a reflection of His
oneness. The mind and the ego think that they have a
separate, individual existence, and create the web of
illusion summed up in the words "I exist." The mystical
path destroys this carefully constructed illusion, until
we realize the truth of God's words spoken to Saint
Catherine of Sienna:

Do you know, daughter, who you are, and who I am? If you know these two things, you will be blessed. You are she who is not; whereas I am He who is.[1]

Only when we renounce our own individual existence can we realize the truth of His existence. The "death" of the ego is central to the mystical path, as expressed in the saying of the Prophet, "to die before you die." This "death" reveals the essential union of lover and Beloved:

If you lose yourself
   on this path
you will know in certainty:
   He is you, you are He.[2]

THE ARENA OF LOVE

For the Sufi the death of the ego takes place in the arena of love. Entering this arena, we turn our back on the values of the world and our instincts of self-preservation. Love is the energy that breaks down our patterns of resistance and transforms us. Love is the energy of oneness in which lover and Beloved are united since before the beginning of time. Deep within the heart there is a place that has no knowledge of duality or separation. The Sufis call this innermost chamber of the heart the "heart of hearts." The heart of hearts is the locus of the spiritual quest, the arena of transformation.

When we say "yes" to the heart's desire for Truth, our consent activates the heart of hearts which starts to spin with the energy of divine remembrance. The heart begins the process of infusing into consciousness the eternal memory of the soul, the union of lover and Beloved, and the knowledge that we belong to Him since before the beginning of time. This is when the confusion begins, because the inner dynamics of the heart belong to a different reality from that of our everyday consciousness. The heart knows neither duality nor the limitations of space and time. The heart is the home of our infinite, eternal Self where we are always together with Him whom we love. Separation is only an illusion of the ego.

The ways of divine love bring the stamp of oneness into a world of duality. While the ego identifies itself through being different and individual, the heart awakens us to an inner reality in which all distinctions merge and all opposites are combined. Within the heart the greatest joy and the greatest sadness are one and the same, death and birth belong together. As the consciousness of the lover becomes infused with this very different reality, the ego's patterns of identity are confused, and the mind becomes lost trying to grasp love's essential paradoxes.

The lover learns to live with states of confusion, with the knowledge that the mind cannot grasp what the heart unfolds. While the mind sees the outer world of appearances, the heart experiences the unity that belongs to the Beloved:

> Reason is like water and love is like fire,
> Water and fire are incompatible.
> In the two worlds, reason sees only the apparent,
> Love only sees the Lover.[3]

The madness of divine love is not just a poetic metaphor but a mystical state in which the lover is thrown beyond the world of reason, beyond the confines of the mind, into the limitless ocean of love. Without form or structure there are no guidelines for the mind to hold onto, no delineations to give us any identity. As the lover is caught in these currents of love, the ego and mind are left standing on the shore. They cannot make the journey beyond the world's end.

The mystic becomes accustomed to bewilderment, does not react to the mind's unknowing. We learn to live without the conditions of thought-patterns and the framework of the ego's identity. Living between the two worlds, we acknowledge the limitations of time and space, but know that our heart is elsewhere, travelling a path without destination:

> I met a woman
> once and asked her where love had led her.
> "Fool, there's no destination to arrive at.
> Loved one and lover and love are infinite."[4]

This infinite path is the ancient journey of the soul. Since the beginning of time souls have been travelling homeward, called by the heart's remembrance, "the sweetness that was before honey or bee."

BEWILDERMENT AND KNOWING

The arena of love is a place of bewilderment, confusion, and knowing. Slowly a truth deeper than reason permeates consciousness. The barriers between the two worlds are broken down by the energy of love, and we learn to live in the presence of Him whom we love.

The ego, which separates us from our Beloved, is strongly identified with our thought-patterns. The bewilderment of the mind is a part of the death of the ego. The more we know about the Beloved, the less we know:

> The more a man or woman knows,
> the greater the bewilderment, the closer
> to the sun the more dazzled, until a point
> is reached where one no longer is.[5]

At the beginning it can be a shock to lose the security of the mind and its structures of self-identity. But the sweetness of love draws us on, beyond the boundaries of self-protection. The lover becomes accustomed to bewilderment, and as the following dream shows, other people rarely notice our inner state:

> In my dream I have lost my head. My neck is healed over like a person who has lost an arm or a leg. I have a party to go to, so I look around for my head. I feel that it might be nice to have it for the party, but it has really gone. I get dressed and notice how easy it is without a head. I look in the mirror and there I am without my head. I have no teeth to brush or hair to comb. All that seems absurd. I go to the party and my friends know who I am. They ask me how I am doing. I say fine but I seem to have lost my head. Someone responds with "Oh, really?" like they were talking about the weather.

The dreamer who has tasted love has lost her head. At the beginning she feels that for the party of everyday life she should have a head. But once love has taken hold of the heart we belong to love and cannot return to the confines of a dominantly mental consciousness. This dream also suggests the simplicity of life without a head, "no teeth to brush or hair to comb." At the party there is no interest in her state, for most people are so identified with their thought-patterns that they cannot even imagine a state of being in which the mind no longer rules.

Our western culture places great emphasis on the mind and intellect. Descartes' saying, "I think therefore I am," is at the foundation of western rationalism. The rational values of the mind support and confirm the ego's illusion of its own identity. These values are now woven into the fabric of our western society. Our collective education trains the mind in the patterns of rational thought and has created a culture based upon an illusion of separate identity. Because the "leaders" of our culture are often those who have excelled in this mental education, we are governed not only internally by our own mental patterns, but also externally by the same limited rationalism. The mystic who knows that "the mind is the slayer of the real" walks a path away from these collective values. We leave behind the security of the collective, to gamble on an inner longing, as 'Attâr describes when he compares reason and love:

> Reason needs a guide who converses,
>   But a sigh which inflames the soul is
>   sufficient for love.
> Reason trains the intelligence and intelli-
>   gence affirms itself,
>   But love is a flame which gambles with
>   the soul.[6]

PAIRS OF OPPOSITES

The ways of love may seem madness to the mind, but they have their own logic. The knowing of the heart is an experience in which there is no distinction between the knower and that which is known. While the mind can only understand through separation, the separation of subject and object, the heart knows through oneness. At first this is usually experienced in dreams where the dreamer experiences a *state of knowing* in which the object of knowledge cannot be defined. This is the higher knowledge of the heart.

The knowing of the heart is beyond duality. This is the wayfarer's destination on the path of love, and paradoxically also where she begins. The first paradox of the path is that "the end is present at the beginning." The wayfarer is then introduced into a world of unity. He who is eternally present reveals Himself within the heart of His lover, and so begins the circular journey of self-revelation. Fakhruddîn 'Irâqî describes how different this is from the ways of the external world:

> Seek not, find not—
> except in this one case:
> Until you find the Friend
> you'll never seek Him.[7]

The seeming contradiction of seeking what you have already found awakens us to the reality of love, the oneness in which everything is contained from the beginning.

This awakening throws us into the arena, where like the gladiators of old we await our own death. Held in oneness, we are torn apart by the contradictions of love. The experience of love's unity demands the death of the ego, the sacrifice of the self, as al-Hallâj expressed in his famous statement, "Kill me, o my trustworthy friends, for in my being killed is my life."[8]

Life and death are the most primal pair of opposites, the first pair of opposites to arise into the consciousness of primitive man. The terrifying goal of the mystic is to embrace these opposites and thus free himself from the chains of worldly existence. Love is a sweetness and a cruelty that can take us beyond ourself:

> When al-Hallâj was in prison, he was asked: "What is love?" He answered: "You will see it today and tomorrow and the day after tomorrow." And that day they cut off his hands and feet, and the next day they put him on the gallows, and the third day they gave his ashes to the wind....[9]

What al-Hallâj experienced publicly on the gallows of Baghdad, each lover comes to experience silently within her own heart and psyche, for "Nothing is possible in love without death."

Life and death stand like two pillars at the final doorway of the heart. But love's path takes the lover through many pairs of opposites. He who is One and alone reveals Himself through opposites, and as we follow the path homeward so we find His unity within duality. At first the opposites seem irreconcilable, and, bewildered, we are thrown between them:

> Sometimes He shows Himself in one way, sometimes in the opposite way—the work of religion is naught but bewilderment.[10]

Sufi manuals have described many different pairs of opposites that belong to the path, for example: fear and hope, chastisement and mercy, presence and absence, awe and intimacy, contraction and expansion, annihilation and persistence.[11] Things can only be known through their opposites. God who has no opposite cannot be known, but through His opposites we can come to know His attributes. Thus Sufis sometimes show the pairs of opposites as a ladder of ascent leading to God who alone is the true *Coincidentia Oppositorum.*

Climbing this ladder, we gradually pass from the outer world of duality to the inner dimension of unity, where the knowing of the heart replaces the knowledge of the mind. The energy of love and devotion is the agent of transformation. The mind and the ego usually resist, fighting the heart with doubts and arguments. The work of the wayfarer is to cooperate with the inner dynamics of the heart, to "walk gladly to the gallows." Although the aspiration and commitment of the lover are the most important factors, it also helps to understand, as far as we are able, the processes of the path. The more we understand the more we are able to surrender the mind. The ultimate realities of the quest are beyond our comprehension, but we can grasp some of the seeming contradictions that confront us.

Because our culture is founded upon rationalism we have to rediscover the fundamentals of mysticism. We have to free ourselves from the constrictions of dualistic thought in order to embrace a reality where beauty and terror coexist, and insecurity is the greatest security. Learning the logic of love, we can see more clearly the guidance of the heart and the pointers on the path of no return. Understanding the inner mean-

ing of apparent paradoxes enables us to appreciate the
subtleties of our inner unfolding, the mystery and
wonder of the journey. Sometimes in order to accept
the difficulties of the path we need to know that

> All is sweet that comes from the Beloved's
>   side—
> It is never bitter if you taste it with care.[12]

THE TWO WORLDS

Attuning consciousness to the inner processes of the
heart, we learn to walk the thin line between the two
worlds. Outwardly we remain in the world of multiplicity, while inwardly the lover becomes more and more
immersed in unity. In the outer world the lover is God's
servant looking always towards her Lord, while inwardly the heart loses itself in the ocean of divine love.
This is the station of "the true confession of Unity:
immersion in the contemplation of God along with the
preservation of the stages of servantship."[13]

Living in the two worlds, we bring the secrets of
the heart into everyday life. The demands of everyday
life require that His servant not be "lost in the clouds"
but reflect the needs of the time. Sufis are not "lotus
eaters," living in the daydreams of spirituality, but
responsible men and women who have tasted the fruit
of oneness. Integrating everyday consciousness with
the inner wisdom of the soul is demanding work,
particularly as the external world in which we live is
dominated by materialism and rationalism.

Working upon ourself, polishing the mirror of the
heart, we learn to see our own qualities from a different
perspective from that of the ego with its distorted split

between good and bad, success and failure. The mind begins to grasp a wholeness in which the opposites form an integral part of a pattern of unfolding. Within this pattern unity reveals itself, for, in the words of al-'Alawî, "Things lie hidden in their opposites, and but for the existence of opposites, the Opposer would have no manifestations."

Gradually the eye of the heart opens and a consciousness founded upon unity is born within the wayfarer. This consciousness of the heart, also known as the higher mind, reflects the oneness of the Self rather than the duality of the ego. With this consciousness we perceive the unity within multiplicity. Experiencing the reality of "Wheresoever you turn, there is His face," the lover sees the Beloved everywhere:

> Everyplace I cast my glance
>   I see You.
> Glory be to God!
>   Have you become my very eyes?[14]

When the ego is surrendered to the Self, the eyes of the lover become the eyes of the Beloved. Through the open heart of the lover, the Beloved witnesses His own creation. Living our everyday life, we silently bring this quality of consciousness into the marketplace of the world.

Our western world has suffered the divisive effects of rationalism to a dangerous extreme. Our planet cries out for an ecological awareness founded upon wholeness rather than fragmented egocentrism. But deeper even than the awareness of one planet and the unity of life is the consciousness of unity that belongs to a relationship with the Creator. The work of the mystic is to live this consciousness, a consciousness born from bewilderment, confusion, and love. The consciousness of unity has an impact on the collective that carries the potency of divine love. Through the open eye of the heart He is able to heal His own world and share His mystery.

EMBRACING THE OPPOSITES

The Sufi does not avoid or withdraw from the contradictions of life. Embracing these contradictions with love and acceptance, we follow them to the source. The ego automatically separates the opposites into good and bad, pleasure or pain. The instinct of self-preservation chooses pleasure over pain and so the ego remains caught in duality and the conflict of opposites. The lover who knows that the pain of love, the heart's longing for God, is the quickest way Home, has a higher priority than self-preservation. She seeks the extinction of the self that separates her from her Beloved.

Embracing the opposites within the heart, we turn away from duality and the dominance of the ego. The heart reveals the hidden face of life's contradictions, in which the deeper purpose of the soul becomes manifest. To bring into consciousness the soul's purpose is to step away from the cycle of life and death into a different dimension, which sees life as a school of learning. In this school there are no such things as good or bad experiences, only experiences. If we reject the experiences that life brings we reject the possibility for growth and inner development. If we accept with love life's difficulties and dilemmas, we cooperate with their deeper purpose. Sometimes in a

dream or intuition we glimpse their meaning, the
lesson we need to learn. Once during a painful period
I had a dream in which I had to teach a child the lesson
of "Absolute Poverty." Spiritual poverty, "having nothing and wanting nothing," means surrendering even
the desire to change a painful situation. This runs
contrary to every instinct, but is central to the way of
the Sufi.

The path bewilders us, turning all our values
upside down. But the potency of love is that it does not
belong to the world of the ego but to the reality of the
Self. Within the circle of love there are no contradictions, no opposites. The power of love frees us from
these limitations, but only if we embrace them. If we
try to escape the opposites we are caught more firmly
in their grip. Love frees us both from the outer world
and from ourself. The mind first becomes confused and
then surrenders to the heart; the ego resists and is then
overwhelmed by a power greater than itself. The
wayfarer may be frightened by this power which does
not separate pain from pleasure, but somewhere we
know it is our only escape. And we are guided by those
who have gone before us, even if they leave few traces:

> In the arena of love do not think of the
>   head—
> Climb on the Beloved's gallows that you
>   may become healed;
> Love is a dragon; those who have been
>   devoured know that![15]

Wayfarers who have entered the heart's arena
know the truth beyond duality. They experience within
their own being how the opposites are held together

by the dual energies of creation, feminine and masculine, *yin and yang*, negative and positive. The two
worlds, the inner and the outer, balance each other,
and, like two mirrors held face to face, reflect eternity.

Life and death are woven together and we are a
part of this weaving. When the eye of the heart opens,
we can see beyond our own individual existence into
the oneness of life and then further into the emptiness
from which life is continually reborn. Non-being gives
birth to being, from which the opposites are created
and life continually manifests. The lover who tastes the
essence of love passes from duality to unity, from
being to non-being. This is the ancient way of the
mystic, of the fool who tears aside the veils of the world
because of a crazy desire to go Home. Lovers are born
into this world in order to break free from duality and
dissolve into unity, yet also to remain here in His
world, carrying the secrets of the heart: how duality
and oneness belong together. Thrown into the world
of separation, we come to know that there is no
separation. In the world of existence we realize our
own nonexistence. Through the opposites we come to
know Him who has no opposite:

> The final and ultimate return of the gnostics…is
> that the Real is identical with them while they do
> not exist…. The gnostic is known only through
> the fact that he brings opposites together, for all
> of him is the Real. Thus Abû Sa'îd al-Kharrâz was
> asked, "Through what have you known Allâh?"
> He replied, "Through the fact that He brings
> opposites together," for he had witnessed their
> coming together in himself….[16]

SEPARATION AND UNION

I want union with Him and He wants separation;
thus I leave what I want so that His wish comes true.

Al-Ghazzâlî[1]

THE HEART'S AWAKENING

The spiritual path begins when the heart is awakened to His eternal presence. The Beloved looks into the heart of His lover and in that instant the lover knows the secret of divine union, that the lover and the Beloved are one. The glance of the Beloved carries the consciousness of His eternal presence.

The Sufis call this glance the moment of *tauba*, the turning of the heart. The inner awareness of His presence turns the heart away from the world and back to God. He calls us back to Him with a momentary glimpse of His face. This glimpse is love's most potent poison that begins our dying to the world, our journey back to God, for "How can I look at the loveliness around me, how can I see it, if it hides the Face of my Lover?"[2]

The inner awareness of union awakens us to the pain of separation. When the heart knows that in its innermost essence it is united with God, we are confronted with our own isolation, with the knowledge that we are separate from God. It is only because we have been given a glimpse of union, had a sip of this divine wine, that we are made conscious of

1

separation. Without the knowledge of union, how could we know that we are separate? Without having experienced the bliss of His presence, how could we know the agony of our own isolation? The pain of longing is born from the glance of God.

From the beginning of the path, the opposites of separation and union are engraved into the heart and psyche of the spiritual wayfarer. The consciousness of union becomes the pain of separation that reminds us of our real Home. The heart's remembrance of its Beloved is kept awake by the fire of longing. We long for Him whom we love, and the greater the love, the greater the pain of longing. Love and sadness become the substance of our inner existence. In the words of 'Attâr,

> The pain of love became the medicine for
>   every heart,
> The difficulty could never be solved
>   without love.[3]

THE POLARITIES OF LOVE

Union and separation, love and longing, sweetness and despair, the polarities of the mystical path leave us bewildered and confused. Why are we left here behind the veils of separation when we know that separation is an illusion? Why are we caught in the prison of duality when our heart knows the deeper truth that "everything is one"? The more we meditate and pray, the more we remember Him whom our heart loves, the more alienated we feel in a world that appears to have forgotten Him. Somewhere we know what it is like to be loved beyond measure, and here we are left in a world where love is too often equated with demands and co-dependency. The eternal question of "Why are we here?" has an added poignancy and poison when we have felt the infinite nearness of our real Home.

He whom we love has abandoned us and only the pain of separation reminds us that somewhere He is "closer to us than our very neck vein." We carry the pain of remembrance in honor of our love, yet only too often we feel betrayed. How can such a Lover desert us? How can such a Beauty veil Her face? Doubts bombard us as the mind tries to convince us of the stupidity of our quest: to look for what you cannot find...to long for an invisible Lover who has only brought you pain.... In many ways consciousness crucifies us on our search. The subtleties of torture with which the mind can torment are known to most travellers on the path of love.

Underlying these difficulties is the fact that while the nature of love is to draw us to union, the nature of the ego is separation. Love comes from the heart, the innermost core of our being which is our connection to the Absolute. Love is "the essence of the divine essence,"[4] and so dynamically pulls us towards one-ness. But the ego is born out of separation. The ego's existence is defined by being different: "I am different from you." The path towards union with God takes us away from the ego with its sense of separate existence and individual identity. This is why the Sufi says that the first step towards God is the step away from oneself. Love calls us to come away from ourself and enter the abyss of oneness where only the Beloved exists.

The ego and the mind belong to a dimension of separation and duality. The ego exists through its sense of individuality and separation; the mind only functions through duality: through comparison and differentiation. The power of love lifts the veils of duality, threatening the ego and confusing the mind. The ancient path of the mystics takes us back to the source where distinctions and differences dissolve just as "sugar dissolves in water." On this journey the ego and mind rebel as their identity and function are attacked. Love draws us into the gladiatorial arena in which we fight our own liberation and resist the pull towards oneness. But those whose hearts are committed know, like the gladiators of old, that death awaits them. They know that they have to lose themselves in order to find their Beloved.

We hide from the love which alone can heal us. We run from the Truth which torments us. But like the encroaching tide, the tremendous power of love gradually smoothes away the ego's paltry marks in the sand. Slowly we come to recognize the infinite ocean as our real Home, an ocean where, in the words of Rûmî, "swimming ends always in drowning."[5]

THE AXIS OF LOVE

Paradoxically, we need the experience of separation to draw us to union. The state of union is the natural state of the soul. The experience of union is the "wine that made us drunk before the creation of the vine." But this secret, hidden within the heart, requires the pain of separation to bring it into consciousness. The pain of love is the effect of the magnetic attraction between the soul and its source. When we feel the heart's pull we feel the desire of the Beloved to become conscious within the heart of the lover:

> Not only the thirsty seek the water,
> the water as well seeks the thirsty.[6]

Separation and union are woven together to form the very fabric of the journey. While the heart knows the secret of union, the ego is stranded in separation. The inner world haunts us with this promise of oneness and the outer world tempts us with so many reflections. These are the twin poles of our existence, what is hidden and what is manifest, the Creator and His creation. The mystical journey leads us along this axis of love, the path from the creation back to the Creator. On this journey we bring the seed of our own consciousness and lay it at the feet of our Beloved. We bring an awareness of separation into the arena of union.

"I was a hidden treasure and I wished to be known, so I created the world."[7] From His solitary aloneness He created the world and brought into play the opposites of day and night, positive and negative, masculine and feminine. In this world He manifested His attributes, His divine Names, the names of majesty (*jalâl*) and the names of beauty (*jamâl*) or the names of severity (*qahr*) and the names of gentleness (*lutf*). These pairs of opposites create the dance of life, the unending dance that comes from the unmanifest, inner world, onto the stage of manifestation. A human being, born onto this stage, is a part of the dynamic interplay of opposites, but at the same time we carry the unmanifest oneness as a memory imprinted into the innermost chamber of the heart, the "heart of hearts."

> Man is My secret and I am his secret. The
> inner knowledge of the spiritual essence is a
> secret of My secrets. Only I put this into the heart
> of My good servant, and none may know his
> state other than Me.[8]

In His world of duality we carry the essence of His
oneness. The work of the mystic is to make conscious
His oneness and offer it back in devotion. Thus we
make Himself known to Himself. Without the stage of
separation this journey would not be possible. It is the
interplay of opposites that reflects His divine Oneness
back to Himself. Without the mirror of creation He
could not see His own face.

THE CYCLE OF LOVE

The wayfarer needs to contain the primal contradiction
of separation and union. Born into separation, we all
carry the seed of union. But in forgetfulness we
abandon ourself to separation, to the world of the ego.
We are so easily lost in the maze of mirrors that forms
His world. Sometimes, as if by accident, we glimpse a
reflection of something other than the ego and its
desires, a hint of a reality behind the veils of manifestation. Sometimes in a dream we are shown a different
horizon where the sun never sets. The Other, so near
and so hidden, haunts us with a memory of oneness
that some call paradise.

Rationally we dismiss these signposts because
they point in a direction other than the goals of our
conscious life. But those whose destiny it is to make
the journey Home are not allowed to forget. The
eternal memory of the soul has been burnt too deep to

be rejected as childish fantasies. The hunger for Truth eventually surfaces, battering on the door of the heart and even affecting the mind. Our world of duality begins to be permeated with a desire for oneness; separation longs for union.

Turning away from the world, we embrace the mystical quest. We respond to the call of the Simurgh, the mythical bird that lives beyond the mountain of Qâf, in the cosmic dimension of the human being. The way there is inaccessible, and only madmen and lovers can make the journey. The Simurgh is so close to us but we are far from him. "Many lands and seas are on the way.... One plods along in a state of amazement, sometimes smiling sometimes weeping."[9]

Following the thread of our own spiritual destiny we walk towards union. We seek what cannot be found, for how can duality discover oneness? In the experience of union all duality disappears. There is neither wayfarer nor goal. This is the state of *fanâ*, annihilation. The lover is lost in the Beloved. Only the moth consumed in the flames of love knows the true nature of fire, but who is left to know? At the very center of her own existence the lover discovers the truth of nonexistence. The manifest returns to the unmanifest and the cycle is completed.

In the journey back to nonexistence, what had been hidden is revealed. The secret at the core of creation is made conscious. But who or what carries this consciousness? If there is no lover, who knows the nature of love? If there is no longer any separation, how can there be consciousness of unity? He who is One and Alone needed creation in order to become known. He needed to create duality in order to reflect His own oneness. The lover needs to remain in duality in order to be a mirror for her Beloved. This mirror reflects His unity both to Himself and to the world. In order to make conscious His oneness the lover has to remain partly in separation.[10] This is one of the most painful paradoxes of the journey.

In meditation I have had the experience of being dissolved into oneness, lost in the nothingness of true being. Here there is the deepest fulfillment and absolute security. Beyond the mind is a belonging in which one experiences one's true nature as it always is. In these moments one is forever embraced by an emptiness that is absolute fullness. These are the experiences one has struggled to reach; they are the fruits of all of one's efforts of meditation and inner work. In the moment of the experience there is no time, no sense of limitation. But then one returns from meditation to be surrounded again by the images of the mind and the identity of the ego. Something so real and infinitely precious seems now only a memory. The ego has drawn its veil and then the world makes its demands. We have worldly duties, a schedule to keep.

When I first experienced being drawn back into duality there was a sense of regret, a longing to remain beyond the ego. Why did I have to come back into the conflicts and difficulties of everyday life, return to a reality which I *knew* to be an illusion? But over the months this regret disappeared. Although every meditation did not take me back into the dimension of true being, sometimes I would be drawn into this emptiness. I came to realize how such an experience is always a gift, given by Him to whom I belong. The experience would remain as long as was necessary, and return when He willed. At the same time I began to understand in my heart how I have a duty to remain here in this world. His gift could only be fulfilled by my returning to duality. There was a joy in coming back to the world with a knowledge of oneness, for I knew that He had shared with me what is hidden within creation.

For Him non-being and being are two sides of one coin, two aspects of His absolute nature. Returning to duality completes the circle of love. What is hidden becomes invisibly revealed, and life manifests its deepest purpose within our own individual existence. For me this revelation was not dramatic or mind-shattering; rather it was a deep awareness of every-thing being as it should be, of a primal meaning being made conscious within the heart. From the heart this meaning and sense of purpose becomes infused into every aspect of the psyche, every cell of the body. Even the mind is included, because as it comes to know its own limitations it also carries a reflection of the beyond.

We desire union but He needs our separation. Surrendering to the spiritual path means to carry the two worlds of oneness and duality. At the beginning this is a crucifixion. We glimpse oneness and yet remain caught in separation. We taste the fruits of union only to be thrown into the experience of separation. But gradually the duality between the two worlds dissolves in the deeper recognition of His oneness. Returning to duality we carry the secret of the heart, the recognition of oneness into the marketplace of duality. Our desire for union is surrendered to His need for separation:

> A thousand times
>   sweeter than Union
> I find this separation
>   You have desired.

In Union
    I am servant of myself,
In separation
    my Master's slave;
and I would rather
    be busy with the Friend
whatever the situation
    than with myself.[11]

The lover longs to be united with his Beloved. But deeper than this longing is the surrender of the lover's soul through which the Beloved can make Himself known both to Himself and to His world. The Beloved needs the lover to carry His secrets of oneness, to be a vessel for the mysteries of love and enable the creation to reflect His hidden Face. The lover is always the servant of the Beloved, and in this state of servanthood there is such fulfillment that surrendering to duality is a joy. The lover desires nothing more than to be used by the Beloved.

The wayfarer walks the narrowest path that runs between the two worlds. In the states of union the lover is lost in the Beloved, and in the states of separation the lover carries His hidden treasure into the world. In love and devotion we renounce union and embrace separation. But because union is the pre-eternal state of the soul and the essence of love, union can never be lost. In love union is always present. In the depths of the heart lover and Beloved are one, as al-Hallâj exclaims:

I saw my Lord with the eyes of the heart
And said: "Who are you?" He answered:
   "You!"[12]

As we live our devotion in our daily life, the heart's knowledge of oneness becomes infused into consciousness. Bringing His secret into the world, we come to know His oneness more fully. As His servant and love's slave we carry both our own separate existence as lover and the knowledge that only the Beloved exists. Existence and nonexistence are bound together in service.

DESIRE AND PROJECTION

Surrendering to separation means embracing the contradictions of the world, the difficulties of the present time and place. Today in the West we live in a culture whose material values appear antithetical to the spiritual quest. The path of the Sufi has always stressed the importance of being an integrated member of society, often "indistinguishable from the crowd." Through our normal outer appearance we are able to work in the world without evoking prejudices or other barriers. Sufism is a path of the householder, living according to the needs of the time and place and the people. In our Western society, where, for example, one may need a car or a computer to make a living, unprecedented material needs are placed on the shoulders of the wayfarer. Embracing the two worlds has never been more difficult.

The work of the wayfarer is to live a balanced outer life while keeping the inner attention on the path and on the needs of the Beloved. Our consumer culture attempts to grip all of our attention with desires and a feeling of unfulfillment that can only be answered by the material world. This material emphasis appears to run counter to the spiritual path, and yet it is so all-pervasive that it cannot be denied. It dominates the collective consciousness of our time.

One way to live in the world and yet be free from the grip of material greed is to discriminate between needs and desires. Needs are what is necessary for everyday life—food, clothing, transportation etc.— and will depend upon our outer circumstances; the needs of someone providing for a family, for example, will be different from those of someone living alone. Because we need to be integrated within our external environment, our judgments of what constitutes a need must be flexible. A woman working in the film or television world in Hollywood, for example, will need to be more fashionably dressed than someone living in a small country town. The wayfarer needs to be free to respond to the needs of the environment.

However, because the pressure of the collective is so strong, it is easy to be caught in the web of desires that permeate our culture. Differentiating between desires and real needs can be an intensive work of discrimination. But if we are honest and sincere, discrimination provides a quality of consciousness that can separate us from the thought-forms of the collective and also from our own greed.

To discriminate between needs and desires is not easy. Nor is it necessary to renounce all desires. Only too easily are desires repressed into the unconscious where they exert an even more powerful grip. Irina Tweedie recalls being on the banks of the Ganges watching the initiation ceremony of some *sannyasins*. In an impressive ceremony these men have their hair shaved; they renounce the three worlds and put on the orange robe of the *sannyasin* (*sannyasin* means "wandering monk without any desire"). The next day Irina Tweedie was bathing in the Ganges while the newly initiated *sannyasins* were sitting on the rocks above the river, using their *malas* and repeating their *mantra, Ram, Ram.* A *sannyasin* is supposed to not so much as look at a woman, but here were two Western women in bathing suits; their arms were showing and their legs were showing. As he said his *mantra* one *sannyasin* kept turning to take furtive looks at the women in the water. Had he renounced anything? No.

On the Sufi path, rather than being renounced, desires "fall away" as we become aware of the real fulfillment that can only come from within. When all you have in the world is a hundred dollars in your pocket, these hundred dollars are very important. But when someone puts ten thousand dollars in your other pocket the hundred dollars lose their importance. When we are given a glimpse of the beyond our values change and the attractions of the outer world begin to dissolve.

Sufism, like Buddhism, advocates the middle way. Living a balanced, everyday life, we use our energy to keep our inner attention on our inner goal, rather than fighting the illusions of the world. We know that our desires can distract us, but we also know that our most powerful desire is to go Home. Focusing our attention on this primal desire is more effective than denying the myriad worldly desires that bombard us. Through focusing on the Beloved we become more and more one-pointed, which in itself frees us from outer distractions.

Sometimes we may need to become conscious of how a worldly desire restricts us, and use the knife of our devotion to become free. But also through looking at the source of a desire we may be able to recognize that underlying every desire is the real need that only He can fulfill. At times, in order to distract ourself from the abyss of real freedom, we cover our longing with the superficial drives of the ego. But more often what we seek in the world is just a reflection of the soul's hunger. Instinctually sensing our own divinity, we long for what is best, for what is perfect. This drive is easily projected onto the outer world, a dynamic reinforced by the external goals of our culture and the progress of technology. We want to have the best vacation, enjoy the perfect stereo sound. We easily become caught in the chase for outer perfection, following the projection of an inner ideal.

The longing for what is perfect, for the ultimate experience, is an important drive and should not be rejected. Through understanding the source of this hunger we can gradually detach ourself from any expectation of external fulfillment. Finally we come to know that perfection belongs only to our inner self, and is reached through a state of spiritual poverty, of inner emptiness. This intangible truth is frightening to the mind and the senses, which try to turn our attention back to the physical world where desires appear to have a tangible goal. Realizing the way we project our inner need, we can turn our attention away from life's stage towards the inner arena of the soul.

LOVE AND PROJECTION

Materialism is not the only source of desire. Human relationships, sex, and the web of romantic love offer us a stage on which many projections can be enacted. In this arena the border between love and desire is more insubstantial. Although the advertising media would have us think otherwise, most of us know that a new car will not bring true happiness. Human relationships, however, reflect the deep need of the soul to be loved. Human affection and love are necessary, and their deprivation can cause psychological and emotional damage. But the spiritual wayfarer is seeking a deeper fulfillment than even the most loving human relationship can offer. How often is this need projected into a human relationship, a relationship which is limited by the very fact that it is human?

In a human love affair the mystery of projection is enacted, as we project onto our partner the inner god or goddess. From the work of Carl Jung and others we have come to understand the psychological dynamics of projection, how our partner can carry the mysterious image of our own inner divinity. In our search for a loving relationship, are we seeking human or divine love? Is romantic love just another illusion that the wayfarer needs to dismiss on the path towards union?

When the heart is awakened, the mind, the ego, and even the psyche are often confused by the consciousness of an intangible, unobtainable experience of union. In the core of our being we glimpse the oneness and yet there is no road there, no visible way to cross from the duality of the ego to the unity of the Self. What we long for we cannot grasp or obtain.

We know that to arrive we must lose ourselves in love, but the reality of an invisible Beloved stands only at the fringes of our consciousness. The experiences of intimacy and ecstasy with the inner Beloved far exceed anything possible with an outer lover, but until we have surrendered into His arms, ecstasy without a visible partner seems too unreal. It is only too easy to project our deepest desire into the tangible world of human relationships. A few months after I met my teacher, my girlfriend of many years left me. I was heartbroken, but soon I had a dream in which I was back together with her. The quality of love and intimacy made me feel that this dream was more than mere wish-fulfillment. I told the dream to my teacher who did not interpret it. Believing in my dream, I waited for my girlfriend to return, which she never did. Only years later did I understand that the dream described an inner experience of intimacy with the real Beloved. I realized that my mind, with no other vocabulary for love, had portrayed this experience in familiar, human images. The one for whom I longed had returned to me.

The mind, unable to grasp hold of an invisible Lover, tries to identify the heart's longing with a human lover. This dynamic can be particularly strong and confusing if at the time we are unfulfilled in our human relationships. As the heart opens to love, and the longing for oneness surfaces, these feelings become caught in patterns of unfulfillment, and projected onto real or imagined love affairs which include the tangible bliss of sexual union.

An added difficulty in this dynamic is that spiritual wayfarers often have a solitary nature that may result in their being unfulfilled in human relationships. An inner orientation towards the Beloved can result in a sense of inadequacy or emptiness in human relationships. Because these individuals instinctively, and often unknowing, look towards God, they can never fully engage in a human relationship. Irina Tweedie called such individuals "branded by God." Just as a farmer brands his sheep or cattle, so does God brand these souls so that they belong only to Him. They often find it easier to love God than to love and give themselves to another person. However, due to the secular nature of our society which has little understanding of an inner love affair with God, those who are branded in this way may live for many years sensing just inadequacy and failure. Only when they finally find their spiritual path do they come to realize the real meaning of their seeming deficiency. Then, like the ugly duckling realizing that he is in fact a swan, they recognize their true nature.

Finding a spiritual path, participating in a spiritual group, the wayfarer gets a sense of real fulfillment. But unfulfilled human desires and longings do not just disappear with the advent of a spiritual path. In fact the energies activated through meditation and other practices may bring unresolved feelings and unlived desires to the surface, which are then easily projected onto the outer world. Does abandoning oneself to love mean following these projections, or attempting to go beyond them in favor of spiritual pursuits? One cannot easily distinguish the subtleties of feelings or hold back from the intensity of passion. Only the heart knows the right path, and often the heart takes us into the turbulent arena of human love to bring us closer to God.

A human love affair dynamically enacts the opposites of our human and divine nature. A love affair offers a stage for many conflicting aspects of our inner self to be enacted. Searching for the divine in another person, we encounter our own psyche, mysterious, alluring, attractive, and destructive. While remaining within the confines of human nature we enter the world of the gods with their passionate and quarrelsome attributes. For the spiritual wayfarer the archetypal world has a particular potency as a doorway into the infinite. Without entering into a detailed discussion of romantic love, I would suggest that the contradic-

tions and the spiritual energy and power of a relationship that opens the door to our deeper self are not to
be rejected.

To quote Jâmî, "You may try a hundred things, but
love alone will release you from yourself. So never flee
from love - not even from love in an earthly guise - for
it is a preparation for the supreme Truth."[13]

Love comes from a single source and is the
greatest power in the universe. Because "love is the
essence of the divine essence", it belongs to unity and
can free us from the grip of duality. Sometimes love
and the power of projection will pull us into an outer
relationship—though for the wayfarer commitment is
never to another person but to love itself, to the
insecurity and ultimate security that belong to the
heart. But not always is the inner drama enacted on
life's outer stage. Often circumstances, responsibilities,
or inner guidance make us contain our feelings. Then,
as with Majnun, our beloved Layla remains physically
unobtainable. But as in the story of Layla and Majnun,
unrequited love does not limit the transformative
nature of the experience. The inner stage can be as
potent or even more powerful, as the lover embraces
the projection with the deeper desire for Truth. But
whether enacted or inwardly contained, in either
instance the heart knows the mystical truth that in
every love affair it is really Him whom we love:

> All love for someone else
> is but a whiff
> of Thy perfume:
> none else can be loved.[14]

THE SHRINE OF DIVINE MYSTERY

The journey Home begins when the soul leaves its state of union with God. Born into this world, we learn to look for our true being and find the way back to our Beloved. He whom we love is veiled by His creation, which both hides and reveals His face. What we usually seek in the outer world is a hidden aspect of our own self, brought to life through the drama of projection. The Sufi learns to use His creation as a mirror, reflecting back both aspects of our own psyche and the beauty and majesty of our Beloved. Rather than rejecting the creation we use it as a means of returning Home, for He has said, "We will show them Our signs in the horizons and in themselves."[15]

There is an Islamic tradition that God gave Adam the knowledge of the divine names reflected in creation.[16] These divine names give man the ability to recognize the essence of creation, the divine aspects of himself and the world. Looking at the world with the eyes of devotion, with the knowledge that only He can fulfill us, we are able to sense His signs. When the heart is awakened it seeks the real Beloved both hidden and revealed in the play of forms. To quote Hujwîrî:

> Know that I have found the universe to be the shrine of the Divine mysteries, for to created things God entrusted Himself and within that which exists He has hidden Himself. Substances and accidents, elements, bodies, forms, and dispositions are all veils of these Mysteries.[17]

We embrace the creation as a reflection of the Creator and as an environment in which we can come closer to

Him whom we love. For the Sufi life itself is always the greatest teacher.

The creation is a mirror of the Creator. When the heart is awakened, the eye of the heart opens, and with this eye the lover is able to read the signs of her Beloved, to see His face reflected in the world around. The eye of the heart is the organ of direct perception, through which we can see things *as they really are* and not *as they appear to be*. When the eye of the heart is closed the world appears to have an autonomous existence, and we are caught in the wheel of life, from birth to death. When the inner eye awakens, the mirage of the outer world changes and we begin to see the hand of the Creator at work. Sensing His presence in the outer world frees us from the world's grip, as we become inwardly aligned with the Creator rather than the creation.

Inwardly the heart turns towards God; outwardly we feel what is behind the dance of forms. Sometimes we see His light in the eyes of a friend, lover, or stranger. In the glory of a sunset we see not just the beauty but the hand of the painter. We catch a whiff of His perfume and know it to be His.

Gradually His signs become visible and we are able to glimpse the thread of our own deeper destiny woven into the outer events of our life. The destiny of the soul is the path that leads us to freedom as we learn the lessons of our incarnation. One friend had a dream experience in which she was lifted up, away from the world, where she was shown that this world is just a play, a stage on which we all enact certain parts. But she was also shown that before we are born we are each given a card of destiny to play, which is also a problem we have to solve. When we have solved this problem we are free to leave, or to stay and help others. There are many clues, signs to help us solve our problem, but we can only see them when we live in the moment. If we live in the past or the future these clues are inaccessible. She awoke from the dream experience with a profound sense of awe.

If we live in the past or the future, in our memories or expectations, we are firmly caught in the illusion of time and the dance of shadows. Only in the present moment do we have access to our eternal Self, which is outside of time. In the intensity of each moment there is no time, as lovers know only too well. Love does not belong to the world of time, but to the dimension of the Self. For the Self, the pre-eternal state of union, the bond of love between lover and Beloved is eternally present. This is the axis of love that is at the core of creation, at the center of every moment. When we experience love we are in that instant attuned to this core. What we feel in our heart is a reflection of His love for Himself.

The path of love takes us away from the web of time, as Rûmî celebrates:

> come out from the circle of time
> and into the circle of love[18]

In love there is only the eternal moment. When we say "yes" to the heart's desire we step "into the circle of love." Then, through our devotion and spiritual practices, the energy of love is activated and we go beyond the limitations of the mind and the illusion of time. In moments of meditation we can experience the infinite space of the heart's eternity. Returning from beyond the mind we may find that we have been meditating for a few minutes or a few hours.

Stilling the mind in meditation, we train ourself to be able to step out of the circle of time. We learn to become conscious in a space where there is no time. But when we return to our daily life we are surrounded by the demands of time, which cannot be ignored. We have appointments to keep, schedules to run. Then through the practice of the *dhikr* we keep our connection with the eternal moment.[19] Repeating His name, we keep awake the memory of when we are together with Him, the memory that is eternally present within the heart. The first *dhikr* was at the moment of the primordial covenant, when in answer to God's question "Am I not your Lord?" the not-yet-created humanity responded, "Yes, we witness it" (Qur'an 7:171). The *dhikr* is the affirmation of His presence within His creation.

His presence frees us from the knots that entangle us here. When the heart affirms that He is One, the chains of duality dissolve. In recognizing that He is Lord we become bound to the Creator and not to the creation. We become His bondsmen, and as Hafîz exclaims, "Only the bondsmen are free." When we see His signs in our daily life, when we glimpse His face mirrored in His creation, we automatically look to Him and not to the world. He attracts our attention back to Himself.

SERVANTHOOD

In the silence of meditation we go beyond the dualities of the mind into the uncreated emptiness where the ego dissolves and the lover ceases to exist. Coming out of meditation we return to the world of separation in which, repeating His name, we evoke His presence, for

He has said, "I am the companion of him who recollects Me."[20] The lover carries the dual consciousness of union and separation. Knowing our essential non-existence, we also welcome our existence so that we can affirm His presence.

The work of the lover, the one who has surrendered herself to her Lord, is to be His representative here. Mirroring Him within the heart, the lover brings His light and love into the world. This light is an inspiration and guidance to those who want to find the way Home, who need to know where they belong. The following dream describes the mystic truth that although one's inner experiences cannot be communicated, the light born from these experiences can help others on their way:

> I am standing at a window looking at the night sky. The sky is deep blue, lit from a full moon not yet risen. I have taken the drug ecstasy, but I cannot tell anyone about the experience. I can only put a candle in the window to tell others.

The dreamer is a therapist and the window in the dream is the window of her office. By doing her work in the world she can make known the hidden and indescribable reality within. The light of the lover's inner being, shining with the radiance of His love, reflects directly into the hearts and consciousness of others.

From heart to heart the secret of divine love is silently told. Words so easily bring confusion and misunderstanding. They belong to duality and are easily caught in the complexities of the mind. The light within the heart communicates directly from essence to essence. Silently, hiddenly, His lovers work in the world, sweeping away the dust of forgetfulness, the darkness of disbelief. Sufis are traditionally known as "sweepers," because they clean the hearts of people. In the words of Shabistarî, "If there were no sweepers in the world, the world would be buried in dust."[21]

Living an ordinary life in the marketplace, His lovers are indistinguishable from the crowd. But within the heart, longing and remembrance create a space for His work to unfold. He needs us here to help keep the world attuned to love, to keep alive the consciousness of His presence. The lover surrenders even the desire for union because the Beloved needs us to embrace separation. In the depths of the heart we come to know the truth of union, but in order to live and work in the world we need to retain consciousness of separation. The seventeenth-century sheikh Ahmad Sirhindî says that the state of servanthood is higher than the state of union, and that the Sufi "chooses separation over union at the command of God."[22]

THE MIRROR OF SEPARATION

His lovers are those who tasted the wine of union before they were born. Yet in that pre-eternal moment of the primordial covenant we surrendered to separation in order to witness Him as Lord. Born into creation, we make the journey of forgetfulness, the journey from God. Then, in the experience of *tauba*, the heart is awakened to its innermost state of union and the lover becomes conscious of the pain of separation. Without the knowledge of union there would be no awareness of separation. These opposites are at the core of the mystical path. The longing for union draws us from the world of duality back to our Beloved. Yet at the same time we feel the soul's surrender to servanthood. We know that we belong to Another and ask that "Thy will be done on earth as it is in heaven."

The desire for union and the need for separation coexist within the heart of the wayfarer. The mystical path is not a linear progression from separation to union to servanthood. It is a spiral in which opposites turn into each other. From duality we turn towards oneness, and in oneness we embrace duality. Thrown between these opposites we experience the "yo-yo syndrome," the swing from nearness to separation that cleanses the heart of the lover. He holds our heart between His two fingers, and sometimes He turns it towards His face and we feel intimacy and awe. Then the heart is turned away and we feel the anguish of abandonment, or the haunting memory of His beauty. Gradually the opposites merge in the center of the heart which is also the still center of the turning world.

Through meditation we come to know that our individual existence is an illusion. In the emptiness beyond the mind we taste our own nonexistence. Returning to duality and the ego we feel the pull of remembrance and come to realize that our need to remember Him is a reflection of His need, our prayer is His prayer. To quote al-Hallâj:

> I call to You...No it is You Who calls me
>   to Yourself.
> How could I say "it is You!"—if you had
>   not said to me "it is I."[23]

25

Our individual existence is just a manifestation of His oneness. The ego's sense of individuality is a reflection of the fact that He is one and alone. Through our "I" we worship Him as one.

Some lovers lost in ecstasy have cried like Bâyezîd, "Under my garment there is nothing but God."[24] They have tasted the truth of their own nonexistence. But when they return from absorption they encounter both their own individual existence and the limitations of this world of forms. Ultimate union is only encountered in physical death; only then was Majnun fully united with his Layla, only at the gallows could al-Hallâj finally realize the oneness his heart desired: "Here I am now in the dwelling-place of my desires."[25]

While we live in the physical world we need to surrender to separation. If it were His will that we always remain fully absorbed in a state of union, we would not wear the clothes of creation. The path of the mystic is to embrace the two worlds, as the Christian mystic the Blessed John Ruysbroeck describes: "He dwells in God and yet he goes out towards all creatures in a spirit of love towards all things.... *And this is the supreme summit of the inner life.*"[26] Within the heart we are united with our Beloved; outwardly we are the servant of His creation.

Initially we may experience regret or even resentment when we return from meditation and have to again take up the clothes of duality. How many times I have wished to remain there, "in the dwelling place of my desires," alone with my Beloved. But surrendering into servanthood we gradually embrace separation *because it is His will.* The resentment passes away, and we remain unattached even to the fruits of meditation. Then, through this state of surrender a wonderful change takes place which the Sufis call *baqâ*, abiding after passing away. *Even in the states of separation a consciousness of oneness remains.*

I had always expected the most significant experiences of oneness would take place in meditation. But, as usual on the spiritual path, things happen differently from the way we expect. A few years ago I moved from London, where I had lived all of my life, to a small town in Northern California. In London I had been living in the same house as my teacher for eleven years, in an apartment above hers. For many years we had over a hundred people a day visiting the house. Moving with my family to California I found myself suddenly alone. Apart from my family I spoke to no one from the beginning to the end of the week. Instead of streets full of people, there were only trees and the ocean. I spent much time alone, meditating, writing, and walking.

The move to California had been at very short notice and had not been easy; my family was having difficulties adjusting to a new life. In London we had been supported not only by the presence of our teacher, but by the many friends in our meditation group, a group which had been central to our life for twenty years. Here we were alone, beginning the work of starting a Sufi Center in California.

But His grace is always present. That winter was part of a six-year drought in California. In England the months of January and February are the most depressing, grey and wet and dismal. Here it was warm and sunny. In January I would walk on the beach, alone in the sunshine. In February spring came, with wild flowers blossoming by the ocean. With the unexpected spring came a new consciousness. Suddenly I found, walking in the woods, an overwhelming sense of oneness. In meditation I had at times glimpsed the oneness behind creation, but now I was experiencing it *in full consciousness.* Wherever I was walking, looking at the multiplicity of nature, the different leaves, trees, flowers, a oneness became visibly present. This oneness was so natural, so much a part of what I saw and felt—it had always been there, only I was seeing it for the first time.

At first I was just amazed and tremendously reassured by this consciousness of oneness. The multiplicity was there, the tide-pools full of creatures, the hawks circling, the star-shaped flowers, but behind and around was this permeating presence. At the beginning I wondered at it, expecting this oneness to be just a passing mystical state. But gradually I sensed its permanence. After writing for a few hours in the morning I would go for a walk, and looking, I found it, both visible and intangible. I sensed and saw the oneness, but not with my physical eyes. An inner eye had been opened.

As the months passed what I had found in nature permeated all of my life. I discovered that whenever I stopped for a moment in the midst of outer activities, I could feel the underlying unity. Interacting with people, or just being immersed in everyday actions, my consciousness would necessarily be caught in duality and the dynamics of the ego. But I came to know that behind this activity a oneness was present, a consciousness to which I could attune myself more and more easily. His companionship became more and more a part of my everyday life. Eventually I would have to try and remember what it was like to live without this quality of consciousness.

Spiritual awakenings are rarely sudden; they develop gradually over the years. It took a number of years for me to become aware of the strength and significance of this new consciousness, to realize how it was the center of my life. At the beginning the oneness was like a warm reassurance, a confirmation that all was well. Whatever the difficulties in my life, I could go for a walk and sense the unity. But spiritual states change, and I had to learn to bring this consciousness more and more into my life. I was faced with circumstances that could not be resolved from the perspective of duality. I needed to fully incarnate this new awareness. Rather than just a reassurance, the oneness became a necessary point of inner focus in my outer activities. I found that if I made decisions based upon duality I got into difficulty. Life was teaching me the need to live from this new consciousness.

Why was I reluctant, at times hesitant, to fully embrace this new consciousness? There is always a price to pay, and on the spiritual path the price is often increasing aloneness. Caught in duality, interacting with life, we are a part of the collective, both supported and also limited by those around us. When I left England I left behind a tremendous outer support, the physical presence of my teacher and the group. I had to stand on my own feet, without outer guidance. I was given a new awareness, but to fully embrace it would also mean fully living my own aloneness, being dependent upon no one outside of myself. The reassurance given by nature's oneness was like a mother's support of her child. But it was not enough just to see and feel this oneness; it had to be lived. I had to become totally dependent only upon Him, His inner presence. The child had to be left behind as I stepped into the bareness and strength of spiritual poverty.

Living from the center of the Self means accepting a degree of aloneness that is difficult to bear. But the journey Home is "from the alone to the Alone." Two cannot walk side by side on this narrowest of paths. Only alone can we come to know His aloneness, His absolute oneness. In meditation we become lost in union, but then we need to live this oneness in our own individual life. Paradoxically we need to live in a state of separation in order to bring His oneness into the world. Accepting oneness also means to accept separation. The consciousness of oneness coexists with the consciousness of duality. The Self and the ego live together.

When we have been lost in union we know that even when we return to separation, separation is an illusion, just as our own ego is an illusion. Separation is a play of light on the waters of oneness. Yet we have to live in this world of separation, just as we have to live with our own ego. The ego remains with all of its limitations and difficulties. We need these difficulties in order to keep our feet on the ground and live a balanced everyday life. Reminding us that we are human, they guard us against inflation. But having surrendered Somewhere we no longer belong to the world or to our ego. Standing alone in the world we are a servant of oneness, living its truth. Surrendering to separation for His sake, we reflect the light of His oneness into the marketplace of the world.

> I and thou signify duality and duality is an illusion for Unity alone is Truth. When the ego is gone [surrendered], then God is His own mirror in me.[27]

INTIMACY AND AWE

*He is and there is with Him no before or after, nor above
nor below, nor far nor near, nor union nor division, nor
how nor where nor place. He is now as He was, He is the
One without oneness and the Single without singleness.
He is the very existence of the Outward
and the very existence of the Inward.*

Ibn 'Arabî[1]

FEAR OF THE TEACHER

For many years each time I came to my teacher's door
I would feel a sense of trepidation and nervousness.
There was no external basis to these feelings, as
generally she treated me with great kindness and love.
But something within me was frightened because I
knew that I was entering the presence of someone who
would do anything for the sake of the Truth. She was
not limited by any of the normal codes of behavior and
all of my patterns of self-defense were inadequate
before her. Sitting in her presence could evoke the
feeling of being in front of a vast empty space in
relation to which my sense of "I" did not matter. My
carefully constructed images of self-value crumbled. I
was totally insignificant, even nonexistent. My teacher
described similar feelings in the presence of her
teacher, feelings of awe and states of nothingness in
which she would pinch herself to feel that she existed.
She also knew that there were no limits, no prescribed

boundaries for this relationship with the teacher. The ego recoils in fear when it is confronted by a reflection of the Absolute. All sense of identity dissolves. Leaving his presence she would run to the bazaar and buy tomatoes to recognize her own sense of taste.

With her teacher she sensed his remoteness, his forbidding look, a hard, cold, stony face. She also felt tremendous love and closeness, an intimacy that was unlike anything she had ever experienced. Her heart would be resting in his heart in infinite peace, despite the people coming and talking to him and the other activities going on. When I dream of her teacher, Bhai Sahib, I feel a deep, deep love, but also an awe that is almost like dread.

The relationship with the teacher echoes the relationship with the Absolute. Within the teacher there is an emptiness of self through which we feel both the intimacy and the remoteness of transcendent Truth. The Absolute is nearer to you "than yourself to yourself" and also beyond what can ever be known or imagined, "beyond even our idea of beyond" (*warâ' l-warâ*). Before the complete transcendence of God the ego responds with devotion and awe. Instinctively the heart of the wayfarer bows down, offering itself to its Master and Beloved.

God, the Beloved, is so close to us and yet so remote. Sometimes He comes with the softness of a lover's touch, but sometimes we feel only our own insignificance. How can we even love that which is so tremendous, infinite? Looking at the night sky, at the overwhelming multitude of stars, we wonder, can the Lord of these worlds also be our own Beloved? How can we reconcile these opposites, His immanence and His transcendence, His tenderness and His majesty? As the heart is awakened to His nearness, so the ego feels

His infinite otherness. We cannot reach Him, only fall in the dust where His feet have been.

PATRIARCHAL DEITIES AND THE REPRESSION OF
THE FEMININE

In our Western Judeo-Christian culture we have been dominated by a masculine, heavenly God. In the Judaic tradition there is an avenging God who banished us from paradise. The God of wrath of the Old Testament was replaced by a Christian God of kindness and love. In the figure of Christ, the Christian God was incarnated, but then ascended from the cross back to his heavenly father. Furthermore, the Old Testament God of wrath remained in the Christian tradition in sermons of hell-fire and the emphasis on human failings and sinfulness. Over the last centuries Puritan and Victorian morality engraved fear rather than love into our religious culture, stressing human inadequacy and leaving a trail of repression and neurosis. How much has this image of a remote and wrathful deity influenced our relationship to the divine?

The masculine divinity belongs to the heavens. Under the dominance of a masculine god, we have developed science and the ability to control aspects of our environment. But we have become separate from the sacred interdependence of creation and no longer live in a daily relationship with the divinity of all forms. Once when my teacher was giving a lecture, she used the term "God's feet." A member of the audience asked, "How can the Absolute have feet?" She responded, "How many feet has a spider, how many feet has a horse?" If God is totally elevated to the heavens it is easy to lose touch with Him in everyday life. We come to know Him only as a distant authoritarian father. Our present culture resonates with the feelings of alienation and individual impotence that reflect the remoteness of our masculine God. We easily feel uncared-for and unprotected, isolated, no longer an integral part of the great wholeness of life.

The sacred wholeness of life belongs to the feminine aspect of the divine, the Great Goddess. For Her every act is sacred; every blade of grass, every creature, is a part of the Great Oneness. In contrast to His awe-inspiring transcendence, She embodies the caring divine presence. The American Indians, among other tribal cultures, honored this aspect of the Great Mother:

> The Great Spirit is our father, but the earth is our mother. She nourishes us; that which we put into the ground she returns to us, and healing plants she gives us likewise.[2]

Like the American Indian, the mystic is familiar with the caring, all-embracing aspect of the divine. Experiences of oneness, which are so central to the mystical path, include every atom of creation; every leaf of every tree is experienced as sacred.[3] One of the first mystical experiences is often a sense of divine presence, and the knowledge of the Beloved's tenderness and closeness grows with our devotion and practices. Like Zuleikha in her love for Joseph, we seek and find our Beloved's name in everything. The practice of the presence of God is essential work for the wayfarer, who shares every activity with her Beloved. Cooking, we stir the pot with Him; walking, we feel Him accompanying us. In difficulty we talk to Him, in delight we praise Him. Repeating the *dhikr* we constantly remember His name with love. We bring Him whom we love into every corner of our life.

In our meditation and our daily life we come to know what our culture has forgotten. We hear the sacred song of divine presence in the marketplace and in our hearts. But we also feel the sorrow of a society that is dominated by a collective sense of divine absence.

Banishing God to the heavens, we lost touch with the sacredness of the earth and its many forms of life. We are slowly becoming conscious of this imbalance and the danger caused by the rejection of the Goddess. We see how our whole planet is suffering from the abuses of masculine technology. At the same time, many patterns of the repression of the feminine have surfaced. Women have had to confront both individual and collective experiences of abuse. The masculine power principle has been recognized as responsible for tremendous feminine suffering, to the individual and to the ecosystem. In response to this deep and dangerous imbalance, the feminine aspect of the divinity, the Goddess, has begun to be reinstated. Reinstating the Goddess means restoring the sacredness of a nurturing, all-embracing divinity. God's masculine omnipotence and transcendence need to be balanced by the feminine aspects of care and nearness.

But we are wrong to restrict our image of a transcendent deity to the patriarchal power-drive. Reinstating the feminine, all-embracing Goddess should not mean denying our instinctual awe for His omnipotence. Nor should the feminine's fear of repression and abuse result in rejecting His majesty. Intimacy and awe are two aspects of God's oneness. The divine is both far and near, as expressed in the *hadîth qudsî*, "My heaven and My earth contain Me not, but the heart of My devoted servant contains Me."

HIS NAMES OF MAJESTY

The obvious difficulty of understanding the nature of God's transcendence is His very transcendence. A *hadîth* states, "Think about the creation but do not think about the Creator."[4] And Sanâ'i has God speak the following words:

> Whatever comes to your mind that I am
>   that—I am not that!
> Whatever has room in your understanding
>   that I would be like this—
>   I am not like this![5]

Yet although God's Essence is unknowable, He has made Himself known through His attributes, His divine names. He has names of beauty, *jamâl*, and names of majesty, *jalâl*. The names of beauty reflect His nearness while the names of majesty describe His transcendence. His beauty is embodied in His creation, as expressed in the *hadîth*, "I saw my Lord in the most beautiful form." In the beauty of His creation God discloses Himself and we can come near to Him. The alleged *hadîth*, "I saw my Lord in the shape of a beautiful young man, with his cap awry," may be suspect in orthodox circles, but it inspired Sufi poets to celebrate the beauty of their Beloved in His creation:

> You look at the beautiful one and see the
>   stature and the figure—
> I do not see in between anything but the
>   beauty of the work of the Creator![6]

But although we may witness Him in His creation, we also know that there is no likeness to Him:

Inasmuch as God is incomparable with all created things, He can only be understood in terms of the attributes denoting His distance, transcendence, and difference. In this respect, human beings sense the majesty and tremendousness of God and perceive Him as Magnificent, Overbearing, Overwhelming, Inaccessible, All-high, Great, Slayer, King. These attributes demand that created things be infinitely far from Him. The things are totally Not He; He is being and they are nonexistence.[7]

In the beauty of His creation we come to know His beauty, while through His omnipotence we recognize that He is Lord and that only He has real existence.

Accepting His omnipotence, we accept our role as slave and servant. He is the ultimate and total authority which we must accept in absolute submission. In the Qu'ran it is said, "He is not asked about what He does."[8] And Rûmî reflects His slave's unquestioning acceptance in his version of Adam's prayer:

If you treat ill Your slaves,
        if you reproach them, Lord—
You are the King—it does
        not matter what You do.
And if You call the sun,
        the lovely moon but 'scum,'
And if You say that 'crooked'
        is yonder cypress slim,
And if You call the Throne
        and all the spheres but 'low'
And if You call the sea
        and gold mines 'needy, poor'—
That is permissible,

for You're the Perfect One:
You are the One who can
perfect the transient.[9]

Only He is perfect, and before His perfection we
can but bow. The total acceptance of what He wills is
a total denial of what we will. "Thy will be done" means
the denial of any self-autonomy except the freedom to
accept His will. He created us in order for us to witness
Him as Lord. The submission of the ego to the absolute
authority of the divine is a cornerstone of every
mystical path. Before Him we are nothing.

When we feel the presence of the divine, whether
in an inner numinous experience or in the presence of
our sheikh, the ego responds in awe or fear. Feeling
His omnipotence, we know our nonexistence. There
have been instances when I have inwardly experienced the power of my sheikh, a power that carries an
absolute authority. My ego senses the overwhelming
power of divine majesty, and any sense of independence or self-autonomy loses its substance. The power
of real spiritual authority is far beyond any projection
onto a father-figure or other psychological power
dynamic. Feeling the authority of my sheikh my desire
is only to obey. There is no possibility of rebellion.
Even later, when the experience has passed, the ego
does not attempt to color the experience with doubts
or distractions. The experience of divine majesty leaves
such a powerful imprint that the ego remains in awe.

In His nearness He is our friend and companion.
In His remoteness He is Lord and Master. These
opposing roles become an integral part of the mystic's
inner relationship with the Absolute. We learn to give
ourself in love and to bow in submission. This duality

of roles is also reflected in the relationship with the teacher, though it can be misunderstood, causing psychological problems. The Sufi path demands surrender to the sheikh, for through surrendering to the sheikh the wayfarer learns to surrender to God. The sheikh can only enact this role because he or she is surrendered to God; the ego has bowed before His omnipotence.

Through the surrender of the sheikh the wayfarer learns to surrender: it is easier to surrender in the presence of someone who is already surrendered. But surrender to the sheikh does not mean unconditionally accepting everything that is said by the sheikh. The sheikh is also a human being with faults and inconsistencies. In fact the Sufi teacher will often consciously show his faults in order to break the patterns of projection and throw the wayfarer back upon himself. My teacher would at times present herself with an old lady's prejudices and inconsistencies and watch to see what reaction it produced. She said, "When people try to put me on a pedestal, I behave badly.... I can swear in English as well as Russian." Although the sheikh will never give a bad example, at times he will put all appearances against him, because the real surrender is never to the sheikh, but to the unmanifest energy of the divine that is present within the sheikh.[10]

SERVANTHOOD AND SERVICE

We easily project psychological problems into our relationship with the teacher and with the divine. In the West our response to His omnipotence can become clouded by both personal and collective attitudes. We live in a culture that values democracy and social equality, and yet the relationship with the divine is one of servanthood and submission. With Him we have no rights, nor is there room for discussion. We aspire to say Yes to God. We learn to do exactly what we are told, not even to try to improve on our inner guidance. Irina Tweedie comments on this:

> And if I receive orders—orders are given by the higher beings who guide our lives—they must be followed exactly.
>
> I cannot change anything. And if my little ego says, "Oh but this is the West and this way will work better," or "For this person this way will not work," it is ineffective.
>
> This is the tradition.[11]

On a psychological level it may be important to clearly differentiate between His omnipotence and any experience of male authoritarianism. Many people, especially women, have suffered from an authoritarian father or other male figures, and many have suffered the collective anguish caused by dominant masculine values. Although it is only too easy to project an authoritarian or remote father-figure onto God, we should try not to cloud our relationship with the Absolute with such psychological problems.

In the state of union we lose ourself in love. In the states of separation we become His slave, standing always in awe of our Master. Once the wayfarer has felt the power of His majesty this awe becomes engraved within the psyche and the mind. There is no possibility for argument or confrontation. The ego may attempt to rebel, but as in the story of Solomon and the gnat, it is confronted by overwhelming force:

A gnat had a quarrel with the wind, and brought his complaint to Solomon. The gnat said that whenever he goes out into the open the wind blows him away, making it impossible for him to reach his desired destination. Solomon listened carefully to the gnat, and then said that he could not make any judgement until the other party was able to present his case. The wind was called, and quickly came to the king. But as he arrived the gnat was swept far away.

The presence of the sheikh, or an inner experience of His majesty, may impress upon His servant the unconditional nature of service. However, this is rarely an instantaneous happening, but rather a gradual process of submission. During this process, psychological resistances will come to the surface. The ego may try to convince us that rather than submitting to God we are just repeating old patterns of abuse or self-denial. What is the difference between the two? Submission to God has a quality of freedom that is not found in psychological patterns. There is a joy in surrender that is very different from the security of co-dependency.

Through the careful work of discrimination and the withdrawal of projections we are able to differentiate between personal psychological dynamics and our relationship with the divine. This is not an easy process, and as projections come into consciousness we may feel that we are even more caught. But in this work we are guided by the light of the Self and by our deep desire to be of service to our Lord. The Sufi bows down before no one but God.

ANNIHILATION AND AWE

For the wayfarer the experience of awe or fear is related directly to the process of *fanâ*, annihilation. The annihilation of the wayfarer can be seen from the perspective of both His nearness and His remoteness. In the states of nearness, annihilation leads to the union of lover and Beloved. The lover's own sense of identity separates him from His Beloved, which made Abû Sa'îd cry:

> Oh Lord God! I do not want myself. Give me release from myself.[12]

In moments of intense love of God there is no difference between the lover and his Beloved: "Lovers do not reach the height of true love until one says to the other, 'O Thou who art I.'"[13] Finally the lover as an individual disappears into the state of union, just as a drop returns to the ocean.

The nearness of the Beloved dissolves the lover, but the majesty of His omnipotence also annihilates us. The following dream experience takes the dreamer beyond personal images of love or closeness into a different arena.

> I am on my way to heaven. I know I am going there. I am in a large hallway, walking. I come to an opening, a large beautiful area with beautiful people. A wonderfully gorgeous man calls to me. I think this must be heaven, but then I know it is not because I am physically drawn further down the passageway. I want to stay, but I must go on. The man comes to me. He is

gentle, kind, and so beautiful to look at. I cannot
stop, for if I do it would be like hell.

I continue to the other end of the hall. It
opens up into nothing. It is like a great void. I
am very frightened, scared to death. Did I make
a mistake? I don't want to go in—there is
nothing there. I am drawn in. I must go in. There
is suddenly an incredible pressure on my chest.
It hurts. I can't breathe. I know that it is the foot
of God. I wake gasping for breath.

The fear felt by the dreamer is the terror of the void, of
the nothingness beyond the ego. In this empty space
she experiences no loving touch but the painful
pressure of "the foot of God." The dream suggests that
in this void she will be unable to breathe, crushed by
His foot. This is the "heaven" to which she is drawn, a
relationship with the divine in which duality is destroyed by His power.

I first met my teacher at a lecture on the esoteric
dimension of mathematics. During the lecture I noticed
a white-haired woman sitting in the row in front of me,
and after the lecture I was introduced to her. She gave
me one look, and in that instant I had the physical
experience of becoming just a speck of dust on the
floor. In that moment my whole self was crushed; all
feelings of self-value disappeared. At the time I did not
understand the meaning of the experience. I was just
left stunned, overwhelmed not by love or devotion, but
by the power of annihilation. Only years later did I
realize that the experience was a foretaste of the path,
of the ancient process of *fanâ* through which the
human being is crushed and destroyed until all that
remains is a speck of dust.

The Paradoxes of Love

An ancient saying holds that we have to become "less than the dust at the feet of the Guru." We have to become nothing, so insignificant that we are just like a speck of dust. Only then can we become permeated with the fragrance of our Beloved:

> A man was walking down a path and suddenly he noticed that the earth where he was standing had a wonderful fragrance.
>
> "Oh dust," he addressed it, "why is it that you smell so nice? Are you a special dust?"
>
> "No," said the dust, "I am just as any other dust, but once a tree stood here and the flowers used to fall to the ground. I was permeated with fragrance, but it is not me, I am just the same dust as any other...."[14]

THE DANGER OF INFLATION

As we walk along the path we begin to glimpse our own divinity, to realize our divine origin. There is an inherent danger in the ego's identifying with this experience, saying to itself, "I am God." Carl Jung called this identification "inflation," and it can produce psychological imbalance. In extreme cases it can lead to psychosis—how often do we read of people claiming to be the Messiah or some other exalted personage, who end up in mental hospitals? On the spiritual path, there is the very real danger of identifying with a numinous or divine experience. Many cults are founded by someone who has had a numinous experience and then feels that he has been chosen by God. The ego, identifying with an inner experience, can have a numinosity that is charismatic, but the dangers are only too well known.

An inner mystical awareness of our divinity, leading to a realization of divine unity, needs to be balanced by the diminishing of the ego. The ego has to be crushed so that it cannot think that it is God. When Irina Tweedie was passing through this stage of inflation, Bhai Sahib looked her straight in the eyes and said, "Only when you become less than the dust at my feet will you be balanced, and only then can you be called a human being."[15]

Only when the ego has surrendered are we free from the danger of inflation. The higher energies of the inner world can then manifest without being caught in ego-identity or corrupted by personal power-drives. When the ego is surrendered it cannot identify with the experiences of oneness. Rûmî tells a story about Bâyezîd Bistamî, the ecstatic Sufi known for his utterances in an intoxicated state of oneness. One night, drunk with ecstasy, Bâyezîd came to his disciples and said, "I am God. There is no God but me. You should worship me." At dawn when he had returned to his senses his disciples told him what he had said. Bâyezîd was horrified at the heresy of his words and told his disciples,

"If I say that again,
bring your knives and plunge them into me.
God is beyond the body, and I am in this body.
Kill me when I say that."

But once again Bâyezîd went into the ecstasy of oneness:

The Light of God
poured into the empty Bâyezîd and became words.

... "Inside my robe
there is nothing but God.
How long will you keep looking elsewhere!"

The disciples drew their knives and slashed out
like assassins, but as they stabbed at the Sheikh,
they did not cut Bâyezîd. They cut themselves.

There was no mark on that Adept,
but the students were bleeding and dying.

.... A selfless One
disappears into Existence and is safe there.
He becomes a mirror. If you spit at it,
you spit at your own face.[16]

Bâyezîd Bistamî was aware of the danger of identifying with the divine, but free from self, he had become just a mirror reflecting His oneness.

Our fear of His might, our sense of awe, remind us that we are human. Bowing before Him, recognizing our role as servant, we are able to contain the heart's experience of union. Knowing that only He really exists enables us to bring His Oneness into consciousness:

> The only thing a person can claim for himself
> is nonexistence, which in religious terms is to be
> God's servant. Indeed Ibn 'Arabî places
> servanthood at the highest level of human

realization. After all it was through his servanthood that Muhammad was worthy to be God's Messenger. Total obliteration before the divine incomparability results in a full manifestation of divine similarity. Not He is simultaneously He.[17]

Confronted by His omnipotence we realize our essential nothingness. Awe evokes intimacy as the ego surrenders, and allows the wayfarer to feel the soul's closeness to its Beloved—His intimacy with Himself is experienced within the heart.

But the function of a servant is to enact the will of his master. As His servant we need to lose all sense of our own self. A speck of dust has no will of its own, but is blown hither and thither in the wind of the spirit. A Sufi prayer echoes this state of selfless service:

> I do not ask to see.
> I do not ask to know.
> I ask only to be used.

We can only be of service to Him if we accept His absolute authority. Otherwise we are just as likely to interfere as to be of any real use. Accepting His authority is not just a mental concept, but an inner attitude of devotion and submission that includes the mind, the body, and the heart. Through this attitude we are able to enact His will in the world, and also manifest the primordial covenant, for with every act we witness that He is Lord.

FEAR AND LOVE

Sufi texts have linked the opposites of awe and intimacy with fear and love (or hope in some texts), and associated them with the dynamic of contraction and expansion. In intimacy and love the heart opens and expands. Fear is a state of contraction that we can feel even physically. Yet, while physical or psychological fear is born from the desire to escape pain or suffering, the real fear of the lover is of anything that may distract him from his Beloved. Fear of God is then not so much fear of His anger but fear of being denied His presence. Abu 'Abdullah ar-Rûdhbârî said, "*Taqwa* (fear of God) is shunning whatever makes you distant from God."[18] And Râbi'a, famous for the intensity of her devotional love of God, never kept a knife in her house "for fear of being cut off."[19]

Carrying the consciousness of this fear keeps our attention on the goal. We fear to offend our Lord, to displease our Beloved. Because this fear belongs to the soul's longing for God it can be confusing for the mind. What is it that we really fear and why does it have such intensity? It is the primal fear of separation, of being denied union. Eventually the surrender of the wayfarer takes him beyond this fear. The wayfarer surrenders even to separation because it is His will. But until we reach this degree of surrender, the inner certainty of knowing that we are in the hands of God, fear binds us to the path.

Fear and love, awe and intimacy, are pairs of opposites that belong to stages of the path. Fear and awe are states of contraction in which we are aware of the ego's insignificance and isolation. Love (or hope) and intimacy are states of expansion when rather than the ego's aloneness, we feel the closeness of the

Beloved, when His beauty, generosity, and grace open the heart. The Sufi masters understood that contraction and expansion need to balance each other. Wayfarers were frequently warned against indulging in one pole at the expense of its opposite:

> Whoever knows God by means of love without fear perishes of [over-]expansion and conceit; and whoever knows Him by means of fear without love is separated from Him by remoteness and alienation; and whoever knows God by means of both love and fear, God loves him and draws him near and teaches him and consolidates him.[20]

"They call their Lord out of fear and love" (Qur'an 21:90). These opposites are the wings that carry our prayers to Him. Expansion and contraction, nearness and separation—the fluctuation between these states transforms the wayfarer, dissolving patterns of ego-identity and molding the psyche and mind into a relationship with the divine that is very different from any human relationship. Through fear and love, awe and intimacy, the wayfarer is remade as servant and lover.

In the presence of my teacher I would experience both fear and love. For many years I longed for the love and recoiled from the fear. I tried to please my teacher so that I would be loved and not experience anger or rejection. But gradually, as my psychological patterns of need and dependency dissolved, I began to experience how fear and love are bound together. The outer dynamic of attraction and repulsion—the attraction of love, the repulsion of fear—changed into an inner belonging to my sheikh. This belonging is so powerful

49

that it transcends the ego. Because I belong to my sheikh I no longer care what happens to me.

The belonging is always present on the level of the soul, but to bring it into consciousness requires a commitment to what is beyond the ego. Living this commitment, the devotee transcends the opposites and the pull of the ego. The lover surrenders himself to the object of his devotion. When the ego surrenders there is no resistance; then fear and love become awe and intimacy. In awe we bow before Him, in intimacy we feel His presence. Awe and intimacy are a part of the soul's belonging to its Beloved, and carry the wonder and joy of this relationship. If you belong totally to your sheikh, totally to the Beloved, only His will matters. There is great joy and freedom in servanthood.

The path of love is endless and the stages change. Sufi manuals, imaging a ladder of spiritual ascent, place the opposites of awe and intimacy at a higher level than fear and love. In the states of awe and intimacy the wayfarer is further from the ego and closer to the Beloved. Awe and intimacy are less dependent upon the wayfarer and more dependent upon God. While fear arises from the anticipation that something will be taken from us, awe is caused by the unveiling of His majesty.[21] Yet even awe and intimacy belong to the being of the wayfarer, who aspires to have existence only in God.

The annihilation of the wayfarer points towards the annihilation of all states. *Fanâ* is followed by *baqâ*, in which the lover experiences that he belongs only to God:

The mystic passes away from what belongs to himself, and persists through what belongs to God, while conversely he persists through what belongs to God, and so passes away from what belongs to himself. [22]

In His oneness all opposites become united, and the being of the lover is infused with the permanence of His presence. Inwardly what remains of the lover is His love; what remains of the servant is His will. Outwardly there remains a shell of separation, a vehicle for His love and His will to come into the world.

The journey Home takes us from the substance of ourself to the substance of God. Through the opposites of fear and love, awe and intimacy, His attributes of majesty and beauty, remoteness and nearness, are impressed into the wayfarer. We are remade to reflect His attributes, to manifest His divine names. In fear we fall before Him, in love we embrace Him. In awe we come to know our own nonexistence, in intimacy we feel His presence. Finally we exist in this world only in servanthood, while within there exists the endless emptiness of His very Being.

The people of perfection have realized all stations and states and passed beyond these to the station above both majesty and beauty, so they have no attribute and no description. It was said to Bâyezîd, "How are you this morning?" He replied, "I have no morning and no evening; morning and evening belong to him who becomes delimited by attributes, and I have no attributes." [23]

LOVE AND VIOLATION

Take me to you, imprison mee, for I
Except you'enthrall me, never shall be free,
Nor ever chaste except you ravish mee.

John Donne

THE RAPE OF PERSEPHONE

The Greek myth of Demeter and Persephone tells the
story of feminine initiation through rape. The maiden
Persephone, also called Kore, is gathering flowers with
her friend when she suddenly notices a narcissus of
striking beauty. She runs to pick the flower, but as she
bends down the earth opens and Hades appears. He
seizes her and drags her down into the depths of the
earth. Kore's mother, Demeter, hears her daughter's
despairing cry for help, and for nine days looks all over
the world. Finally, on Hecate's advice, she goes to
consult Helios, the sun, who has seen the abduction
from his chariot in the heavens. Helios tells Demeter
that the narcissus was planted by Zeus, who planned
her daughter's abduction by his brother Hades, so that
she might become Hades' "flowering bride."

In her inconsolable grief Demeter withdraws from
Olympus and takes refuge among the cities of men. She
comes to Eleusis and has a temple built for her where
she retires into her sorrow. As she withdraws, so the
earth dries up and withers, the sap of growth departs
and the land lies dying. The gods, seeing that without

crops the entire human race will perish and there will be no one to worship them, come to Demeter to entreat her to come out and restore the earth. But she will not permit the earth to bear fruit again until she sees her daughter. Finally Zeus commands Hermes to descend into the underworld and tell Hades that he must return Kore, who since her arrival in the underworld has taken the name Persephone, to her mother. Before returning, Persephone, yielding to Hades' temptation, eats a few pomegranate seeds, a symbol of marriage and fertility. Having tasted the fruit of her womanhood, Persephone must henceforth spend a third of each year with him.

This myth enacts the archetype of the maiden's initiation into womanhood, the dark rite of passage that is a transformation to a greater wholeness. When Kore returns from the underworld she is reunited with her mother into the single figure of Demeter-Kore, who is then symbolically joined by Hecate, the figure of intuitive feminine wisdom. Thus through her abduction, the innocent maiden becomes mother, maiden, and sybil all in one, embodying the three-fold nature of woman made whole.

Helen Luke, commenting on this myth, says that in seeing the narcissus, Kore is caught in the intoxicating moment of seeing herself as a person for the first time, glimpsing her own feminine beauty separate from her mother. Inevitably, Luke says, rape must follow, for

> the moment of breakthrough for a woman is always, symbolically, a rape, a necessity, something which takes over with overmastering power and brooks no resistance.... Any breakthrough of new consciousness, though it may have been

maturing for months or years out of sight, comes through a building up of tensions which reaches a breaking point. If the man or woman stands firm with courage, the breakdown becomes a breakthrough into a surge of new life…. The Lord of the Underworld is he who arises bursting forth from the unconscious with all the tremendous powers of instinct. He comes with his immortal horses, and sweeps the maiden from the surface life of her childish paradise into the depths, into the kingdom of the dead. For a woman's total giving of her heart, of herself, in her experience of her instincts is a kind of death.[1]

New consciousness bursts through from where it has been germinating in the depths. We are carried into transformation, caught by an instinctive drive that pulls us away from the ego into the vaster dimension of the Self. Identifying with the ego, we feel the fear of the unknown and the grief for what is lost, the security of old patterns. These patterns often have to be broken by force, by the shock of the numinous power that belongs to the beyond. Otherwise we would remain forever caught in what has become familiar.

When we are ready, the instinctual energy of the divine invades our carefully constructed identities and ego-patterns. Kore, intoxicated by the narcissus, is inwardly ready to be ravished. She has come to the end of maidenhood, and needs to be taken into the darkness of initiation, the unknowing of transformation. Like children, we are afraid of the dark, but only in the darkness, in the unknown, is there the pomegranate seed of rebirth.

PIERCED BY SPIRITUAL PASSION

The story of Persephone, like all stories of death and rebirth, can be read on different levels. The transformation of maiden into woman embraces the ancient rites of fertility, the immersion in darkness that leads to new growth, that are central to the cycle of life. The maidenhead of innocence must be broken for the deeper mysteries to be enacted, for life and consciousness to be reborn. Conception only happens in the darkness of the earth, of the womb, of the psyche.

The mystic passes through many stages of transformation, many descents into darkness and openings into rebirth. The ladder of spiritual ascent forces one into the depths, and the relationship with the divine Beloved is rarely a gentle courtship. When Rûmî fell at the feet of Shams, caught by a glance from the wanderer's eyes, his whole world of theological knowledge was shattered in an instant.

Violation is a cornerstone of the mystical journey, as the potency of the spirit shatters the ego. The glance of the divine, whether seen in a teacher's eyes or experienced through some other medium of awakening, pierces through to the soul where it sows the seed of spiritual conception. In this moment the imprint of remembrance is activated with enough force to carry us beyond our conditioning and lead us to our death. The sharp sword of divine longing is not just a metaphorical concept, as those who have felt its pain can testify. We are pierced by the passion of our own hidden devotion and by the intensity of the Beloved's need for His lover. We are violated by our love for Him and His love for us.

The paradox of spiritual violation is that it carries the sweetness of a lover's kiss, the potency of intoxication. We are embraced by His tenderness as much as we are broken by His strength. These opposites working together remake us in the mold of love and submission. This is the inner drama of our own rape and dismemberment, in which the mystic is destroyed and remade, loses himself to find His Beloved.

Yet we live in a culture which, having lost sight of the mysteries, equates violation only with destruction and not with rebirth. Having closed the door to the inner worlds, we see only half of the cycle of transformation. Just as we have lost sight of the symbolic meaning of incest,[2] so we have become conditioned to reject the transformative meaning of rape. Enacted on the inner stage of the soul, rape or "ravishing" is a purifying and transformative act, often a necessary part of initiation. The horror we rightly feel towards the brutality of physical rape[3] should not blind us to the potency of its symbolic reality. We need to differentiate between outer human relationships and our inner relationship with the divine. In order to help free ourself from the collective rejection of the sacred we need to reclaim an understanding of violation's link with love.

CONFUSING A HUMAN AND A DIVINE RELATIONSHIP

Confusion can easily arise from our lack of understanding of the difference between an outer, human relationship and the inner relationship with the divine. During a workshop, a young woman shared a long and complicated dream full of confusion. But underneath all the confusion was a real conflict about her relationship to the Beloved. The dreamer had been brought up to believe that in a relationship she should not give herself away but preserve her identity. She should not allow herself to be used, but keep a sense of her own worth and value. She should be aware of her own needs in the relationship, rather than just trying to fulfill the needs of her partner. However much she loved another, she should remain independent and free.

In reaction to centuries of patriarchal repression, these values of self-assertion have become a strong influence in our Western collective, particularly among women. They are an important safeguard against patterns of male dominance and feminine abnegation, but can become a hindrance in an encounter with the inner lover. The relationship with the divine requires total subservience and self-sacrifice. The heart's true Beloved should be approached with a vulnerability in which all patterns of self-defense are laid aside. The lover is worthless, only the Beloved matters; we seek to respond to all of His wishes with no thought for our own needs. "The Beloved is living, the lover is dead" is not only a description of union, but also an attitude of the heart in which the lover looks only to the Beloved.

The dreamer is right to protect her sense of integrity with her boyfriend, but not in her search for God. In the outer world of duality our sense of individual worth is of tremendous importance. We are protecting our human dignity, which is ultimately our own sense of being sacred and whole. Only when we value our own inner self can we offer it back to the Beloved. The Sufi is never a doormat to others. We bow down only before Him.

However, the relationship with God does not belong to the ego but to the Self. In this relationship our sense of self is just an obstacle:

> Oh Lord God, everyone has some wish,
> whereas I want to have no wish. And everyone
> has an "I," whereas I want to have no "I."
> What I want is not to be me![4]

The ego does not need to be protected but rather to be pushed aside, surrendered in the service of love. The embrace of the Beloved can be experienced as a violation of the ego, which loses its sense of self-autonomy. The energy of love devastates patterns of ego-identity. In Sufi symbolism, the "tavern of ruin" is the site of that devastation, and it is there we will find the treasure we seek:

> Wherever there is a ruin, there is hope for
>   treasure—
> why do you not seek the treasure of God
> in the wasted heart?[5]

In our search for human love we seek care, warmth, tenderness, and understanding, as well as passion. We want something for ourself, to hold onto, to give us a sense of self-worth. But the relationship with the Beloved needs a space empty of desires, where the ego does not intrude. The energy of divine love creates this empty space, creates the place for love's meeting in which there is no lover, only the Beloved. A friend describes how during meditation she experienced the power of this love that attacked her mind and ego, destroying everything she thought valuable:

I feel a great field of energy around me which seems to flatten my mind. I start to say a prayer but the words grow fainter and fainter, as if disappearing into a tunnel. Everything I have done up to this point in meditation seems altogether useless within the current of this energy. All of my efforts seem to be selfish and built out of mind stuff, so that they do not survive the extinguishing of the mind. I cry during the entire meditation, seeing everything collapse that I think valuable. Then I am suddenly drawn into a feeling of love wrapping all around me, and so much greater than myself that it is difficult to feel intimate with it. It is like being in a painfully tight embrace, so much that I cry out from the feeling of pressure.

He destroys those whom He loves. Love is the greatest power in the universe and the most destructive to the mind and the ego. Rûmî tells a story of someone who came to the Prophet and said, "I love you."

"Be careful of what you are saying," said the Prophet.

Again the man repeated, "I love you."

"Be careful of what you are saying," the Prophet warned again.

But a third time he said, "I love you."

"Now stand firm," said the Prophet, "for I shall kill you by your own hand. Woe unto you."[6]

Love is a sword of death cutting us loose from the ego. Only when we forget ourself do we remember Him. Only when we have nothing left to lose does He come to us. Then, secretly, unexpectedly, He reveals His presence, the intoxicating oneness of union. Within the heart there is no me and you, no sense of identity or individuality, just a merging and melting into His embrace. Because the ego is the only obstacle, the only protection we need is from ourself. Contrary to all patterns of conditioning, we need to allow ourself to be naked, vulnerable, violated, to be pierced through to the core of our being, to the inner sanctum of the soul.

The energy of love not only attacks ego-patterns; it also opens us. Cutting through the barriers of protection, love reveals the hidden places of the heart. In a human love affair this is where violation and betrayal leave their most dangerous wounds. Scarred by pain, only too often we close ourself, build a defensive shell and repress our feelings. Instinctively we withdraw, safeguarding ourself from further pain. But those who are caught in the grip of longing have to make the dangerous journey beyond the confines of self-preservation. The madness of love is not just a poetic metaphor, but a passion that defies the primal instinct of self-protection. In the words of Rûmî:

> Love comes with a knife, not some shy question,
> and not with fears for its reputation!
>
> …Love is a madman,
> working his wild schemes,
> tearing off his clothes, running
> through the mountains, drinking poison,
> and now quietly choosing annihilation.
>
> …Let the cords of your robe be untied. Shiver
> in this new love beyond all above and below.[7]

Surrendering to violation, we sacrifice ourself on the altar of our longing. We pawn away our own self-worth in our addiction for love's wine. We *know* that love's pain is also its greatest promise. The Self can never be hurt by love. The only suffering of the soul is when we deny the Beloved and turn from His face. In the arena of love only the ego is wounded, only the ego suffers. When there is no obstacle, how can there be pain? Pain is caused by resistance, by the ego struggling to preserve itself or protesting its wounds.

The lover looking towards her Beloved acknowledges suffering but is pushed by a deeper instinct than self-preservation. Once the fire of longing is ignited within the heart, we are caught by the soul's desire for union. When we say "Yes" to the call of the Self we open our heart to the pain of separation. This pain draws us into love's arena where the energy of the Self is stronger than the ego's pull. The energy of the Self does not belong to this world of duality where "I" must protect myself from "you." The Self is a state of union in which "I" and "you" are experienced as a part of the Great Oneness. The only betrayal is when we close our heart to the pain of separation, when we protect ourself from the violation of His touch.

WHAT IS MOST PRECIOUS MUST GO

Being open to violation means to hang naked on the cross of our own longing and suffer the destruction of our beliefs and values. What is most precious to us must go. And while outer attachments may be difficult to give up, beliefs and our own sense of identity are much harder. It is far easier to give up possessions than to surrender ourself. We each have our own particular beliefs, in justice, for example, or our image of what is right. But such beliefs belong to this world and are limited. "Beliefs can be great traps. They can imprison us."[8] There even comes the time when the belief in the teacher has to be surrendered, as expressed in the Zen saying, "If you meet the Buddha on the road, kill him." The wayfarer is walking a road beyond all form, all limitation, into the limitless ocean of His love.

The ego needs an identity, but the wayfarer aspires to being "featureless and formless," an empty mirror that can reflect His light. For many years I was attached to being a spiritual seeker. This was an identity that gave me a sense of purpose and a support in time of difficulties. For a while it was a necessary crutch, but there came the time when it was dissolved and I was left with a feeling of abandonment. What was I if not a seeker? At this time I had a dream of seeing my own coffin on which was written "spiritual aspirant."

Sometimes attachments and identities fall away, sometimes they are torn from our bleeding hands as we struggle to keep a sense of self. We are often surprised by what we find to be most precious, most difficult to lose. But the energy of the Self is relentless in its drive for Truth. If we are attached to being an artist we may lose our creativity. If we are attached to being a failure we may be forced to be successful.

The potency of divine love is that it is not attached to any form, nor will it allow itself to be limited. The work of the lover is to co-operate with the process of destruction, the work of annihilation. Love cuts through illusions and attacks patterns of self-interest. The sword of love is merciless, destroying anything that stands between lover and Beloved:

A bedouin was asked, "Do you acknowledge the Lord?"

He replied, "How could I not acknowledge Him who has sent me hunger, made me naked and impoverished, and caused me to wander from country to country?"

As he spoke thus, he entered a state of ecstasy.[9]

Protecting ourself from love's sword is to protect ourself from His closeness. He empties us of ourself so that He can reveal His beauty and His majesty. Empty and free from self, the lover is open to the bliss of His presence.

DESPAIR AND DEVOTION

His love for us ignites the primal pain of longing, the wound that can only be healed by His touch. The anguish of the soul calls out, awakening us to separation. The potency of this pain is that there is no shelter or defense that can protect us. Our love for Him pierces our patterns of resistance. The hunger for God is no idealized feeling, but a need that comes from the instinctual depths of our being. We crave His touch with a desire only addicts can understand. Caught in love's trap, we would pawn everything, including our self-respect. Love has its own values, as in 'Attâr's story of a lord who lost everything for his love for a beer-seller.

A lord sold all that he possessed—furniture, slaves, and everything, to buy beer from a young beer-seller. He became completely mad for love of this beer-seller. He was always hungry because if he were given bread he sold it to buy beer. At last someone asked him: "What is this love that brings you into such a pitiable state? Tell me the secret!"

"Love is such," he replied, "that you sell all the merchandise of a hundred worlds to buy beer. So long as you do not understand this, you will never experience the true feeling of love." [10]

While human love may offer us security, warmth, a sense of being wanted, divine love opens a different door. The gods abduct Persephone, carry her off to the underworld, leaving a world devastated through her mother's grief. Divine love, erotic and untamable, destroys all plans of prosperity, all images of freedom. The lover is gripped by a passion that is more powerful than reason, her whole being impregnated and then torn by desire. She is like Mirabai, the sixteenth-century Indian princess and mystic who left her palace and wandered the roads and forests searching for Krishna, her "Dark Lord," willing to give up everything for a glimpse of her Beloved.

> Hear my plea, Dark One, I am
> your servant—
> a vision of you has driven me mad,
> separation eats at my limbs.
> Because of you
> I'll become a yogini and ramble
> from city to city
> scouring the hidden quarters—
> pasted with ash, clad in a deerskin,
> my body wasting
> to cinder.

I'll circle from forest to forest,
wretched and howling—
O Unborn, Indestructible,
come to your beggar!
Finish her pain and touch her
with pleasure!
This coming and going will end,
says Mira,
with me clasping your
      feet forever.[11]

The desperation of divine love is that the lover is the victim of a force beyond her control. In human love we engage in power dynamics and strategies of seduction. We play a myriad of games and psychological dramas with our human partners. Whether we assume the role of innocent, hero, temptress, or tyrant, unconsciously or consciously we plan and enact our moves. Patterns of power and protection are woven into our romances and relationships. But with the Beloved we are always a victim.

Whether seduced or attacked by His love, whether we try to run away or give ourself gladly, He is the master and we are the slave. His glance is so potent that we are left helpless. Even when we struggle and fight, we are already love's casualty. With our free will we can reject Him, turn away from the abyss of His embrace back to our problems and attachments, but He remains love's master.

This is no love affair of equals, no give-and-take of partners. Blindly we give ourself to a Beloved who demands total submission, a blank check of devotion. All we have to offer is our incapacity to love Him as He should be loved, our inability to know Him. Silently we plead that He allow us to come close, that He grace us with the merest glimpse from His eyes, the faintest scent of His presence. Like Mirabai, we know that our only place is at His feet.

PREGNANT WITH GOD

On the Sufi path the relationship with the Beloved is reflected in the relationship with the teacher. The sheikh is the mediator between the wayfarer and the Beloved. The heart of the sheikh is a pure mirror reflecting the light of divine love into the heart of the lover. This transmission of love happens on the inner plane of the soul, creating a relationship of impersonal intensity. A friend had a vision of the power of this love when she first came to her teacher's group:

> I had no more than closed my eyes to begin meditating when I saw, indelibly impressed upon my inner sight, the teacher standing before me completely naked and with an immense erect phallus. At the same time his body stance seemed to be similar to that of the Virgin Mary in paintings, where she stands in shy humility, with her legs and feet in a particularly feminine attitude. Thus he stood just looking, his eyes blazing forth at me an unspeakable love that pierced my heart like the blade of a sword.

The friend describes her response to this experience, and her understanding of its implications:

> This vision was a demonstration of the totality of the commitment that would be demanded. It showed that nothing would be permitted to be

held back. But at that moment I knew only that it profoundly disturbed me and threw into chaos all my concepts about spiritual life. It awakened with one gaze from the Divine Lover a longing which tormented me in a way I could not ever get any purchase on. I felt dimly that it might be a numinous event, but it frightened me badly, and I had little conscious context for it. It seemed even sinful, humiliating, and it horrified my mind. All I wanted to do was to run from it as far as I could, block it out of my consciousness forever.

"The body is included," my teacher told me directly afterward, for he had perceived something of what had happened to me, though of course I did not tell him anything, and he knew that I did not understand that all of the seeker goes on the path. Only later I began to understand that the vision of the teacher held out the potential of both the masculine potency of the Higher Self to penetrate and impregnate the soul with divine love and the soul's feminine attitude of nakedness and receptivity before God.

Those of us who have been reared in a tradition that knows concepts and ideas about God cannot even imagine at the outset how completely the lover will be taken by the Beloved in this total love affair. We might know that if we embark on a so-called "spiritual path" we are supposed to share ourself with God, but it is quite a shocking fact to learn that it is not only the best parts He desires, but all of us. Most especially He wants everything of us which we imagine is "not spiritual," and particularly those dark and instinctual parts we feel the need to suppress and conceal. But somewhere in us we do know what He wants, unconsciously, and it is that fateful secret which draws us to this path of love—our overwhelming need to be taken by God. We would never be satisfied with anything less than the whole because He cannot. Somehow it is completely necessary and completely natural to us; otherwise we would not be attracted against our better judgment and good sense to this strange, strange path of love.

The teacher's phallus and nakedness image the potency and vulnerability of the relationship with the divine. The association of the teacher's body with the Virgin Mary points to the immaculate conception, the process through which the spirit impregnates the soul with the seed of higher consciousness. In this vision the impregnation comes from the eyes of the teacher which blazed forth "an unspeakable love that pierced my heart like the blade of a sword.... It awakened with one gaze from the Divine Lover a longing which tormented me in a way I could not ever get any purchase on." The sword of longing pierces into the very core of our being, where the mystery of divine conception takes place: the soul is made pregnant with God. In the words of Rûmî, "Sorrow for His sake is a treasure in my heart. My heart is *light upon light*, a beautiful Mary with Jesus in the womb."[12]

The divine consciousness conceived within the heart of the lover is the knowledge of His oneness, of His unending presence and limitless love. The consciousness of His unity dissolves all semblance of duality, and is a direct perception from essence to Essence. Abû Sa'îd ibn Abî-l-Khayr terms this consciousness *sirr Allâh*, the consciousness of God which God places within the heart. He describes how it comes into the heart:

> *Sirr* is a substance of God's grace and it is produced by the bounty and mercy of God, not by the acquisition and action of man. At first, He produces a need and longing and sorrow in man's heart; then He contemplates that need and sorrow, and in His bounty and mercy deposits in that heart a spiritual substance which is hidden from the knowledge of angel and prophet. That substance is called *sirr Allâh....* It is immortal and does not become naught, since it subsists in God's contemplation of it. It belongs to the Creator....[13]

The pain of longing purifies the psyche and prepares the soul. Longing is the heart's most terrible wound through which we are opened to God. Its intensity enables it to penetrate throughout our being and burn away our impurities. The greater the longing the faster the process of purification. Each atom cries out for union, and as longing permeates our whole being, so is the whole of our self prepared for His embrace. He wants all of us, and not just what we identify as spiritual. The body too is included in the annihilating ecstasy of love. Everything is to be surrendered and given to Him—the mind, the psyche, the body, and the soul. The depth, passion, and intensity of this yielding belong only to divine love, as another friend experienced in meditation:

> I experienced a sudden, intense feeling of being penetrated far into the body. This experi-

ence carried with it a kind of knowledge which is impossible to translate. The power to yield to this love, to allow it to find the darkest places within matter, which it passionately desires to go to, to allow it to illuminate and fill the opening spaces, and to enclose and hold this love at the same intensity of passion, suddenly and joyfully discovered to be identical in some deep, unknown way—this power recognizes and completes a shared desire, springing back as if from long ago, only remembered at the moment of yielding. The feeling in this experience was close to pain. I was holding and nourishing in my body the most exquisite, unknown presence, and my body folded around it in deep pleasure, almost unbearable at first, but changing to a gentle warmth. All other sexual experiences are bland by comparison.

The ancient memory of divine love is made conscious as the lover yields to its penetrating and illuminating power. The shared desire of lover and Beloved belongs to the memory of the soul, to the eternal moment in which "He loves them and they love Him." The incarnation of this experience, felt in the body, the psyche, and the soul, is the completion of the circle of love. To quote Mechthild of Magdeburg:

And God said to the soul:
    I desired you before the world began.
    I desire you now
    As you desire me.
    And where the desires of two come together
    There love is perfected.[14]

The heart's desire for God is born from His love and returns us to Him. Just as love has no limits, longing is not limited. Longing is love's violation, for it does not acknowledge the protective barriers of conditioning, and its pain batters down our resistance to God. Awakened in the core of our being, it is like a traitor in the midst of our ego-self. The more we turn towards God the stronger we feel its pull. Longing is intensified by meditation, and the *dhikr* impresses into us the anguish of being separate from Him whose name we repeat. Our only defense is to deny Him. But then we deny the love our own soul has for its Beloved.

Love and longing violate reason. Love is a madness, a disease, and an addiction. Longing is a sweet poison that brings despair. The heart cries, the soul cries, but He whom we need is absent. We are forced to give away everything, driven by a drunkard's desire for the taste of annihilation. Only love can redeem love's sorrow, and only when we have been permeated by love's sorrow does the Beloved take us. Finally, in the depth of our longing and despair, we give ourself unconditionally. No longer seeking protection, we sell ourself as love's slave to our master. In the words of the fourteenth-century Indian mystic, Janabai:

> Cast off all shame,
> and sell yourself
> in the marketplace;
> then alone
> can you hope to reach the Lord.

> Jani says, My Lord,
> I have become a slut
> to reach Your home.[15]

THE VEILS OF GOD

We are veiled from Thee only through Thee.

Ibn 'Arabî[1]

ALL IS HE, ALL IS NOT HE

"The world is no more than the Beloved's single face," writes the poet Ghâlib.[2] In moments of oneness the mystic glimpses the union of the inner and outer worlds. He whom we love reveals Himself in His creation. The lover is amazed at the beauty of her Beloved, and is caught in the intoxication of the moment. But then the moment passes and we are left with the memory of His presence. His oneness remains imprinted within the heart, but consciously we are confronted with the dance of duality, the *maya* of creation.

The beauty of the world is a reflection of His beauty. Like sunlight reflected in a dewdrop, His light catches our attention. We cannot see His light directly; we would be blinded by its intensity. His creation is a veil of protection, as expressed in the *hadîth*, "God has seventy veils of light and darkness; were they to be removed, the Glories of His Face would burn away everything perceived by the sight of His creatures."[3] Although He is so near to us—"We are nearer to him than the jugular vein"[4]—He shields us from the overwhelming intensity of His nearness. He protects us from Himself with His creation, and yet the mystic longs to lift these veils of illusion, to see behind the dance of creation.

In the moment of *tauba*, the turning of the heart, we are awakened to a reality that is not found in the outer world. Glimpsing His oneness, we recognize the illusory nature of this world of multiplicity. The mystical path is a journey from separation to union, from multiplicity to oneness. We are taught to turn our attention inward, away from the duality of the outer world to the inner dimension of the soul, the hidden chamber of the heart where lover and Beloved are united. The Sufi refers to this innermost space as the "heart of hearts," and here the truth behind the play of forms is revealed.

In meditation we learn to enter this sacred space, taste the bliss of the soul, and realize our primordial state of union. Here there is no form, no feature. Beyond the mind there is a dimension that knows neither limitation nor definition. The heart has no boundaries because it contains the secret of His presence, as expressed in the *hadîth*, "Heaven and earth contain Me not, but the heart of my faithful servant can contain Me."

In the heart of hearts the Beloved reveals His essential nothingness. The mystical truth is that there is neither lover nor Beloved, neither creation nor Creator. The void is the startling reality that every mystic must encounter. Underlying creation is an astounding emptiness, darker than the space between the stars. All images of God are dissolved. There is only an ever-expanding emptiness which throws the mind and ego into a state of confusion near to madness. Who or what is revealed? Who or what is hidden in this revelation?

Turning inward, we turn away from the many towards the one, to the single source of our being. But we find no benevolent Creator, no caring or merciful God. We are lost in a state of nonexistence that is beyond being. In this emptiness there is no revelation because there is no one present. His Presence can only be understood as a state of total absence, as illustrated by the story of al-Hallâj when he was in jail awaiting execution:

> On the first night of his imprisonment the jailers came to his cell but could not find him in the prison. They searched through all the prison, but could not discover a soul. On the second night they found neither him nor the prison, for all their hunting. On the third night they discovered him in the prison.
>
> "Where were you on the first night, and where were you and the prison on the second night?" they demanded. "Now you have both reappeared. What phenomenon is this?"
>
> "On the first night," he replied, "I was in the Presence, therefore I was not here. On the second night the Presence was here, so that both of us were absent. On the third night I was sent back, that the Law might be preserved. Come and do your work."[5]

His Presence can only be characterized by total and absolute absence, both absence of self and absence of any form of God. "There is nothing but nothingness."[6] Returning from this emptiness, the mind only registers not knowing. He whom we so ardently sought reveals the truth that we can never know Him.

"No one knows God but God." But we can experience the emptiness that is a reflection of His essential non-being.

THE DEATH OF THE EGO

God's essential nature is non-being. The wayfarer cannot experience this fundamental truth because

> Man has no access to the domain of Absolute Unity, that station in which God is One in every respect and no other can be conceived or imagined. The Essence remains inaccessible and unknowable to every created thing always and forever.[7]

But, as Chittick points out, the goal of the traveller is not to know the unknowable, but to become "the perfect servant." Becoming the perfect servant is a journey of annihilation in which we lose all sense of independence and separation, and return "to the root of the root of our own being," which is nonexistence. In this state we are united with God to such a degree that we no longer exist, for "God is, and nothing is with Him."[8] Union with God is an experience of our own nonexistence.

Experience of God cannot be reported because there is no one there. The mind, the ego, and all faculties of consciousness are left behind. Bâyezîd Bistâmî came close to describing this state when he said that the third time he entered the Holy House he saw neither the House nor the Lord of the House, by which he meant, "I became lost in God, so that I knew

nothing. Had I seen at all I would have seen God."
'Attâr, telling this story, adds the following anecdote:

> A man came to the door of Bâyezîd and
> called out.
> "Whom are you seeking?" asked Bâyezîd.
> "Bâyezîd," replied the man.
> "Poor wretch!" said Bâyezîd. "I have been
> seeking Bâyezîd for thirty years, and cannot find
> any trace or token of him."
> This remark was reported to Dhûl-l-Nûn. He
> commented, "God have mercy on my brother
> Bâyezîd! He is lost with the company of those
> who are lost in God."[9]

Although we have no access to the reality of
nonexistence, returning from beyond the mind we are
left with a residue of the soul's experience. The
knowledge of our own non-being permeates into
consciousness, reflected from a different dimension.
Bâyezîd, speaking with the certainty of one who has
been "lost in God" for "thirty years," knows the truth of
his own nonexistence. The mystical path is a gradual
awakening to this reality. Even before we cross the
threshold of non-being we may be given glimpses, as
a friend experienced in meditation:

> I am standing on a rock. The rock is sur-
> rounded by emptiness. A wind is howling around
> me and I know that the next step is to jump off
> the rock into the emptiness.

This experience was so terrifying that the friend tried
to forget it for many years. Only later did he realize that
it was a foretaste of truth.

The knowledge of our own non-being is a startling revelation which liberates us from the control of the ego. How can the "I" be the controlling factor when we become aware that the "I" does not exist? Inwardly, beyond the mind and the senses, the higher knowledge of non-being permeates consciousness. The autonomy of the ego is subtly subverted by this deeper reality. Of necessity it happens gradually; otherwise the ego would be shattered and the wayfarer would go mad. But there comes the time when we come to know that the ego is not our real self. Often this revelation comes to us in meditation when we do not need the ego to function in the outer world.

Meditation is a technique that enables us to transcend the ego and the mind. Initially we feel the invisible presence and effect of the beyond. But as our meditation deepens we can develop a consciousness of what is beyond the ego. Then we come to *know* the illusory nature of the ego. Going into meditation I have had the experience of leaving the ego and then *seeing* my own ego-consciousness as a separate entity like a small planet in space, a planet which seemed two-dimensional. Experiencing the vastness of space and the expansion of my true being, I saw how the ego was quite separate and self enclosed, a world unto itself. I knew that I was not my ego, could never be my ego. Ego consciousness looked so limited, defined by such a small parameter compared to the vastness of inner space which was the home of my real being.

As the inner experience became deeper and richer I left the ego far behind. But then, coming back out of meditation, I felt myself returning to this "planet," this small, constricting identity we call the ego. Then I felt myself slipping into ego-consciousness as one would slip into an old suit of clothes. I was aware that once again I was "becoming" this familiar identity with its self-image, its mental patterns, its limited horizon. I saw how easily the ego blocked my experience of a deeper reality, drew a curtain over the vastness of my inner being. I experienced both the constriction and the comfort of this familiar self, this "I." Finally, fully awaking out of meditation, I was back in the ego, with the knowledge of the experience just at the borders of consciousness.

One of the difficulties of integrating an inner experience is that the ego and the ordinary mind are organs that enable us to perceive only this world. They do not have the capacity to allow us even to remember the other reality. As we step back into the ego, the inner experience is cut off. Initially this is necessary in order to live a balanced, everyday life. There are many people in mental hospitals whose powerful inner experiences could not be contained, making them unable to function in the outer world. I once met a woman who had had an intoxicating experience of divine unity. She had seen the oneness of everything, the divinity of the dog-shit on the sidewalk. But because she was unprepared, the experience had unbalanced her. Unfortunately she had been taken to a doctor who had diagnosed her as manic-depressive, and prescribed electric-shock treatment and then anti-depressants. By the time I met her she had been so conditioned into believing herself to be manic-depressive that she could not be convinced otherwise.

A spiritual path and its practices both evoke and contain such mystical experiences. As we progress on the path we develop a quality of consciousness that is strong enough to embrace the two worlds, enabling us to bring an inner experience into everyday life. Through meditation and other spiritual processes we develop the function of the "higher mind" which enables us to remember and integrate the experiences of our real nature.

Using the higher mind to remember what we really are, we bring into ordinary consciousness the truth of the ego's non-being. We know that we are not what we call "I." In our everyday life the ego remains as a vehicle of consciousness, a vehicle which we need in order to function in the world. But gradually it ceases to be *the center of consciousness.* This is what is meant by the "death of the ego."

DISCRIMINATION AND PURE BEING

An inner sense of Self and its quality of consciousness enable us to experience how the ego is an illusion. Reciprocally, as the power of the ego lessens, the wayfarer is more receptive to the consciousness of the Self. While the ego is dominant, the Self remains in the background, as in the image from the Upanishads of the ego and Self as two birds on a tree, one eating the fruit of the tree, the other looking on. One cannot be guided by the Self when held in the grip of the ego. A friend was told this quite clearly in a dream: "People with a strong sense of ego cannot live a guided life." Of course the ego is very clever and can easily pretend to be the voice of the Self, enacting its will under the deceptive guise of "inner guidance." Learning to discriminate between the voice of the ego and the voice of the Self is a cornerstone of the path.

Discrimination enables us to recognize the truth of the Self and the cunning of the ego, but only when we have been absorbed beyond the mind and the ego are we able to surrender to the Self. Irina Tweedie asked

her teacher, "Bhai Sahib, when will the self [ego] go?"
He answered, "When the smaller merges into the
Greater, will the self go."[10] At another time he described
to her the relationship between the ego and the Self:

> "One day the self will go, then only love will
> remain.... You will not say: I love. Where will
> the 'I' be?"
>
> "But how could one live without the center
> of the 'I'? There would be no consciousness, like
> in sleep, for instance."
>
> "Yes, one lives in the self; in my case I can go
> out of the body at any time. When in the body
> the self is present, one suffers, feels like every-
> body else."
>
> "But your self is not the same as others. It
> must be of a different quality."
>
> "The Real Self belongs to the soul; once one
> is established in it, the life on the physical plane
> becomes of small, relative importance."[11]

When the wayfarer has tasted the truth of nonexistence, the ego ceases to be the dominant factor. A
quality of being emerges from within the heart to
become the focal point of life. This quality of being
does not belong to the ego but to the Self. It is a reflection
of His being: "God is, and nothing is with Him."
Initially experienced in meditation or at the moment of
emerging from meditation, the consciousness of being
gradually becomes present in everyday life.

The pure sense of being that can be experienced
in meditation brings into daily life a quality of consciousness that is as different from the ego as formlessness is from form. The consciousness of the Self can be
described as an attitude of receptivity to the divine

hint, but a receptivity that is not passive but highly dynamic. The Self is a state of surrender to the divine will that is simultaneously united to the divine will. The Self is an emptiness merged into His emptiness that is experienced as a dynamic center of being. When the ego surrenders to the Self, this different quality of life becomes present within the psyche, life that is directly dependent upon the Creator and not the creation.

Centered upon the Self, the wayfarer lives both inside and outside the veils of creation. The Sufi master Bhai Sahib says that "when in the body the self is present and one suffers, feels like everybody else," and yet "the life on the physical plane becomes of small, relative importance." On the level of the ego the wayfarer retains a sense of individual identity, and yet knows within the heart the essential illusion of this sense of separateness. On the level of the Self the awareness of our own unique nature comes from our closeness to Him, the clarity with which we reflect His uniqueness. Because He is one and alone, beyond comparison, we feel His divine uniqueness within the heart.

HIS NAMES AND ATTRIBUTES

From His Essence of non-being He brought forth being: "God is, and nothing is with Him." We can never know His Essence, but the "death" of the ego opens us to the experience of divine being. We feel it inwardly in the heart of hearts, and see it outwardly reflected in His creation, as expressed in the Qur'anic saying, "Whithersoever you turn, there is His face (2:115)."

The experience of nothingness awakens us to our own nonexistence and also to the truth of the emptiness that underlies creation. As we come to know that the foundation of form is nothingness, the veils of illusion become insubstantial. How can we be fooled by the dance of illusion when we have experienced this underlying emptiness? Both the outer world of forms and our own ego cease to be hard reflecting surfaces; they become permeated by divine being.

He is always present: "He is with you wherever you are" (Qur'an, 57:4). In the words of Ibn 'Arabî, "The Real is perpetually in a state of 'union' with existence."[12] When we are caught in the ego we are only aware of our own illusory existence. But as the ego loosens its grip we become aware of His divine being. We experience His union within the multiplicity of forms. The veils that hid Him from us become veils through which we come to know Him.

When our consciousness is ruled by the ego we see through the eyes of the ego. The outer world, reflecting the ego, is a veil of separation, a desert in which He whom we seek is absent. Looking for the oneness within the heart, we see the world as a diversity of forms which distract us. The veils which prevent us from seeing God "alert us to the fact that God is hidden behind them."[13] This is why we turn away from the outer world and make the traveller's journey inward. The fruit of this journey is the consciousness of the Self, which gives us the knowledge that "everything is He."

But with the awakening of the Self the ego is still present. There is a period of confusion as the ego and the Self each present us with a different consciousness of the same reality. Before we are fully centered in the Self we are thrown between the two worlds, between oneness and multiplicity. The poet Fakhruddîn 'Irâqî poignantly expresses this confusion:

> If You are Everything
> > then who are all these people?
> And if I am nothing
> > what's all this noise about?
> You are Totality,
> > everything is You. Agreed.
> Then that which is "other-than-You"—
> > *what is it?*
> Oh, indeed I know:
> > Nothing exists but You:
> but tell me:
> > Whence this confusion?[14]

Existence and nonexistence, multiplicity and oneness: which is real and which is illusion? How can there be any illusion when everything is He? When He has revealed Himself, who remains? What is the ego when there is consciousness of oneness? But gradually the confusion clears as the veils of separation become the veils of revelation. Because we cannot know Him in His essential non-being, we come to know Him reflected in His creation. "I was a hidden treasure and I wished to be known, so I created the world."

The Sufis have described the world of forms as "secondary causes," which are understood as outer forms of inner realities. These inner realities are His names and attributes, the qualities of God by which the lover comes to know the Beloved. In the words of Ibn 'Arabî, "God discloses Himself to the lover in the names of engendered existence and in His Most Beautiful Names."[15] But these inner realities, His names and attributes, are obtainable only to those who know that the world of forms is a veil, an illusion. For those who believe in the reality of the outer world, their forms are an obstacle to truth:

God established the secondary causes and
made them like veils. Hence, the secondary
causes take everyone who knows that they are
veils back to Him. But they block everyone who
takes them as lords.[16]

Once the traveller has gone beyond the world of
forms and knows them to be veils, they can reveal their
secrets. Through the interplay of the two worlds, His
qualities, His names and attributes, hidden within
creation, come to be known.

THROUGH HIS VEILS WE COME TO KNOW HIM

The *shahâda,* "*Lâ ilâha illâ llâh*" (There is no god but
God), describes the process of turning away from the
illusion of the outer world where He is absent, "*Lâ
ilâha*" (There is no god), towards the inner reality of
the heart where He is present, "*illâ llâh*" (but God).
Negating the outer world of forms, we affirm His
formless inner presence. But this dualism of negation
and affirmation is only the first stage of the *shahâda*.
The process of separation is followed by a deeper
union which affirms that nothing is other than He, "*Lâ
ilâha illâ llâh.*"

Through the negation of the world of forms and
the affirmation of the heart's truth, the wayfarer comes
to realize that He is eternally present. "He is with you
wherever you are":

> ...Thou has named Thyself the "Manifest"
> and the "Nonmanifest."...
> So Thou art the veil. We are veiled from Thee

only through Thee, and Thou art veiled from us only through Thy manifestation.[17]

Through His manifestation He first veils and then reveals Himself. When the lover has passed from the manifest to the unmanifest, he realizes the truth that he can never come to know His Absolute nature, as the Prophet affirms in his prayer to God: "We do not know Thee as Thou should be known." In the unmanifest, the lover is dissolved into unknowingness. Returning to the manifest, the lover comes to know the forms of the Beloved, and behind the forms realizes His qualities. Through His veils we come to know Him.

Each wayfarer makes his own journey behind the veils and then realizes within himself and within the world the qualities of his Beloved. In His own unique way He reveals Himself to each of us, for "He never discloses Himself in a single form twice or in a single form to two individuals."[18] Each traveller can only tell his own tale. On my own journey there were many years of turning inward. Each time I came to our meditation group I would retire to a corner in silence, not even understanding the need of other friends to talk. The conversation, dreams, and experiences of others passed me by. What was shared I cannot remember. There was within me instead a hunger, a need and despair that drove me inward. I noticed neither others nor how I was with others. Only later did I understand the importance of the community of friends, of talking, laughing, telling stories, of being together in companionship. I also realized that my behavior could have been seen as unbalanced and even rude in the disregard I had for others. However, the group had an understanding and tolerance that belong to those whose commitment is to the path. In fact each of us will at some time pass through a stage when we have no desire for outer communion, and may even positively dislike relating to fellow wayfarers.

But gradually a change happened within me and the focus of my attention was no longer turned so definitely away from the outer world. Possibly two experiences which I had in meditation were a significant part of this transition. One was the first time I consciously awoke somewhere else, to find myself in the presence of my teacher, who handed me a key. It was such a real experience that I was quite shocked when I came out of meditation to realize that I was in my teacher's meditation room, and all the time I had been meditating, my teacher had, on the physical plane, been in her kitchen next door talking and having tea with friends. When I told her of this experience she just said that it was "very auspicious" and that a key is an important symbol. Now I see this first experience of awakening on a different plane of consciousness as a turning point. In *consciously knowing* that I was not limited to everyday consciousness I had been given a key to the door to the beyond.

The second important experience was of being loved totally and absolutely. I had just slipped off in meditation when I felt for a moment within my heart a love so complete that nothing more could be desired. Like a butterfly's wings touching the edge of my heart, love was present, and I knew the truth of Rûmî's words:

> subtle degrees
> of domination and servitude

are what you know as love
but love is different
it arrives complete
just there
like the moon in the window[19]

Just an instant's touch within the heart and I *knew* that I was loved with a completeness that cannot be found in the outer world. The totality of the love included everything within me. This moment of love changed my life, in that I found the absolute security I had been seeking. I could now live without the insecurity that had haunted me. The outer world no longer carried the threat of incompleteness.

The first instance of His touch carries the beauty of a first love. Other experiences of His love have followed, deeper and more intoxicating. But in that first moment everything was present and the foundation of my life in the world was changed.

These two experiences imprinted within my consciousness the knowledge of a freedom and wholeness that are not dependent upon the transient outer world. The hidden remembrance of the heart had been confirmed. Grounded within this absolute security, I was able to return to the world of forms with an affirmation of His presence within my consciousness. And because our experience of the outer world is a reflection of our state of consciousness, the outer world then began to reflect this inner reality. In the forms that had hidden Him I came to know His qualities.

THE FRAGRANCE OF HIS PRESENCE

Before, I had looked for Him unknowingly. I had sought His being in everything. In the early mornings I had walked among the fields as the sun infused the horizon with pink and then red. I had sensed something hidden in this beauty, in the cobwebs of dew spangled with sunlight. Sitting beside a stream I had watched the water tumble among the rocks and felt a stillness behind this movement, a peace in the swirling eddies of water. But I did not know Whom I looked for. Seeing His face reflected everywhere, I did not recognize it.

Falling in love, I felt the truth of Rûmî's words that:

> a woman is God shining
> through subtle veils[20]

and like the firefly was drawn into the flames of Her beauty, the mystery of Her passion. I was intoxicated by the shimmering light of these veils, the tumbling locks of her hair and depth of her eyes. As in the imagery of Sufi poets, I was caught, entangled in the bewitching wonder of Her form:

> My heart on your tresses' twists
> Was caught, not just my heart,
> My soul too, in the same crux
> Became entangled.[21]

But on the journey of negation I was turned away from these forms, from these entanglements, from the reflection of His face. My heart was torn away from any outer attraction, from the grip of *maya*. Returning, I sensed both the veil and Him whose beauty had entranced me. I marvelled at Her mystery, the feminine side of God that holds the intoxication of wonder. At the same time I was free of the entrapment, the longing to find Her in Her forms. I knew that holding Her reflection would not fill the vacuum of my heart. Beauty's bewitchment, in which we are held captive by creation's illusion, was past. Knowing She was elsewhere, I could love Her reflection without desiring it.

"The Prophet loved perfume, beautiful women and the shining of eyes in prayer." The fragrance of the Beloved can be found in many places. He comes to us through the mystery of His forms, through images which carry the secret of remembrance. To each of us He comes in our own way, according to our nature and temperament. Some see His face in the eyes of hungry children or in the need of the sick. For the artist He may make Himself known in the paintbrush or in the feel of wood. For some He is visible in nature, or in the wonders seen through a microscope. Although I have experienced His oneness in nature, honored His beauty in His creation, and felt the truth of Ibn 'Arabî's words that "Woman is the highest form of earthly beauty,"[22] for me dreams have been the most visible imprint of His presence.

Dreams embrace the images of the outer world and yet have a translucence that belongs to the beyond. In my own dreams I sensed His presence long before I consciously knew Him. Drawn into the practice of dreamwork, I found myself involved in the dreams of others, and here I found His footsteps most visible and came to know Him better.

There are many different types of dreams, and only some come from the spiritual dimension of our being.[23] These dreams carry an atmosphere that belongs to our transcendent Self, which makes Itself felt in the telling of the dream. Through the dream a quality of the Beloved is reflected into consciousness. He has many different names and attributes, and different dreams reflect individual qualities. He may appear as the majestic beauty of a range of snow-capped mountains, or the subtle beauty of a flower. He can come with the power of a tremendous storm, or the absolute authority of the Self whose voice must be unquestioningly obeyed. He has the strength of an elephant and the lightness of a feather. Sometimes He comes with the sweetness and softness of a lover's touch, as in the following dream image:

> Suddenly a slim and delicately built woman appears, dressed in a simple orange-yellow robe. I take her in my arms, kiss her, and the taste is wonderfully sweet.
>
> I lie down with her and we melt into each other. Her body disappears in a second as a wave of sweetness, bliss, and peace pulsates like a wind through my whole being.

The same Beloved can appear in another's dream as a man whose eyes carry the frightening quality of eternity:

> I feel a sense of danger, some man who wants to come into my house. I close all the windows and shutters of my house. But when I go to the back door it is open and a wind is blowing into the house. I know that a dangerous man is inside, but I don't see him. An artist in the house is able to make a sketch for the sheriff. He

sketches a ghostlike figure in which all that can be seen are two piercing eyes that seem to go on forever.

While He may come to the soul with sweetness, to the ego He can appear in the guise of a dangerous intruder. The soul embraces eternity but the ego recoils in fear. The wind of the spirit belongs to the beyond, and it brings the knowledge of His power before which the ego is always afraid.

The presence of the Beloved can evoke both sweetness and fear. He also has the quality of aloneness which all wayfarers come to experience within themselves. The following dream evoked this aloneness, and brought a sense of desolation which is a human response to the absolute nature of His solitariness:

> I was floating in the sea after a shipwreck. At a distance from me were many other bodies also floating after the shipwreck. They were making no effort to swim and I knew that the current would not take them to shore. Eventually they would all drown. I was not making any effort to swim, but I was in a different current which slowly took me to the shore. When I came out of the water onto the shore I realized I was totally alone. Not just because I was the only survivor, but there was no one else in the whole land. I felt totally and desolately alone.

The shipwreck of the ego leaves the dreamer in the current of the path. This current will take her to a different shore, the aloneness of the soul. In the words of al-Hallâj, "God is solitary and loves the solitary. One,

He loves only him who witnesses Him as One."[24] In our aloneness we come to know His aloneness.

In listening to these dreams, one can hear the echoes of the footsteps of the Beloved walking across the hearts of His friends. The traceless path of love comes in many forms. He appears and reappears, glimpsed through the veils of the stories of love. Sometimes when a dream is told the room fills with the silence of His emptiness, or the joy of His kindness. There is laughter at the way He tricks us, how we are fooled by His cunning, diverted from the roads of reason by love's seduction. Or a dream full of longing will touch the hearts of those present, reminding us of the endless journey that is our commitment to Him.

WATCHING THE WORLD FOR HIM

Hearing travellers' tales, we all share in His mystery. The lover comes to know of many of the variations of love, the tender ruthlessness of our Beloved, the intoxication and terror He can leave behind Him. We learn to expect the unexpected, to be deceived and to love the deception, to be confused and embrace the confusion. Walking between the two worlds, we become attuned to His hidden music. We allow ourselves to be led beyond all boundaries, to stand on the edge of the world, as a friend experienced in meditation:

> I am at the edge of the world. On my left side is the world, all full of light. On my right side all is dark and black. Out of the darkness pure love comes into the world. At this moment I know that this is His game and I have nothing else to

do but play it by His rules as He wants. It is His game and I have to play it as He wants.

I experience a great longing to go into the darkness, but I realize that I have to wait until He takes me inside the darkness. Until then my job is to wait at the edge of the world and give everything I see to Him.

This dream carries the imprint of the ancient mystical path of devotion and service. Standing at the edge of the world, we belong to the beyond, to the darkness to which we long to return. As the "doorkeepers of love" we wait where love flows from the uncreated emptiness into creation. We watch the world with the eyes of those who have seen its illusion but remain within the circle of life. We see not with the duality of the ego and its patterns of avoiding pain and seeking pleasure, but with the detachment of devotion. We play His game of life according to His rules, from the perspective of the Self that waits at the edge of time.

Sufis are known as "a brotherhood of migrants who keep watch on the world and for the world."[25] We learn to watch with the eyes of Him whom we love, of Him who has touched our hearts and turned them towards Himself. He has awakened our hearts so that He can use them to see His face reflected in His creation. Having pierced our hearts with the pain of longing, He sees through the opening. We are a veil that has been made transparent.

Such is the glance of God that if He were to look at His creation directly it would burn and disappear, for "the Glories of His Face would burn away everything." The servant is God's hearing and sight. Through his devotion "the servant is the hearing and seeing of the

Real…. For God looks at the cosmos only through the
sight of this servant, and the cosmos does not disappear."[26] Such is the nearness of the lover and Beloved
that we are used so that He can come to know Himself.

As He reveals Himself to Himself, so He leaves in
the heart of His servant an imprint of His qualities, of
His names and attributes. The qualities by which He
reveals Himself reflect the individual nature of the
servant. Through our own nature we come to know
Him. We cannot each know all His names.[27] For some
He is *Al-Muqît*, the Nourisher, or *al-Wasîc*, the All-
Comprehending, or *Al-Musawwir*, the Shaper of Beauty,
or *Al-Matîn*, the Forceful One. According to tradition
He has ninety-nine names, and as He wills He reveals
them to us, according to our own nature. In revealing
His names He reveals the essential qualities of our own
being, as suggested by the saying, "He who knows
himself knows his Lord." We come to know Him as He
is reflected in our own unique self. And as we come to
know Him so we come to know ourself not as a veil of
separation, but as a veil that carries an imprint of His
face.

When the ego is absorbed into the Self, the servant
is born. The ego bows down before the Self just as the
Self bows down before God. This is the moment of
transition when the veils of separation become the
veils of revelation. In the awareness of our own
essential nothingness we lose the need for the identity
of form. The veils of the world become permeated by
His light, infused with His fragrance. The two worlds
merge together, first within the heart and then within
consciousness. As the eye of the heart opens, the
servant realizes that "The eye through which we see
God is also the eye through which He sees the

world"—in Ibn 'Arabî's beautiful image, the friend of God is "the pupil in the eye of humanity."[28]

Pure Being is unknowable, and has neither name nor attribute. Only when it gradually descends into manifestation do names and attributes appear. The names and attributes carry the inner meaning of the created world, which becomes visible to those who see with the eye of devotion. The diversity of the created world "is the outward aspect of that which in its inward aspect is God.... But the Absolute cannot rest in diversity."[29] This outward spiral into life is balanced by the inward spiral of the journey Home, in which form returns to essence. When the wayfarer returns Home he brings back knowledge of His names and attributes and lays it at the feet of his Lord. In the heart of the servant the Absolute becomes conscious of Itself.

Returning Home, His servant carries within his heart both the unknowable essence, the emptiness that is before and after creation, and the secrets of creation, the qualities of God. The deepest secret within the heart is hidden even from the knowledge of His devoted servant, for it is too esoteric to be known. This secret is carried within the core of the soul until the soul merges forever in union. But a reflection of this secret is carried in the consciousness of love, in the lover who by penetrating the veils of this world has come to know through those veils some of the qualities of his Beloved.

TWO WINGS TO FLY

God turns you from one feeling to another
and teaches by means of opposites,
so that you will have two wings to fly,
not one.

Rûmî[1]

THE MASCULINE AND THE FEMININE PATH

Everything that comes into manifestation has a dual aspect, positive and negative, masculine and feminine. Even the primal energy of love has a masculine side, "I love you," and a feminine side, "I am longing for you." The spiritual journey itself also has a masculine and feminine nature. The masculine aspect of the journey is the path from multiplicity to oneness, in which we turn away from the veils of illusion to seek the inner reality beyond form. In the previous chapter I described how through this journey of turning away from the outer world we complete the circle and come to know Him whom we love reflected in His creation.

However, for the feminine He is always present. The feminine embraces the deepest secret of creation in which the Creator and His world are eternally united in love. The feminine path is to make conscious this instinctual link of love, this bond born outside of time. For the feminine the circle is always complete because the nature of the feminine is wholeness. Her work is to bring the circle of love, the natural wholeness of the Self, from the instinctual world into consciousness.

Yet because the outer world involves the limitations of time and space, its divisions and dualities, the feminine fears the violation of her instinctual wholeness. Within the psyche and understanding of the feminine there is no separation, only the sacred oneness of life and love, but the outer world continually confronts her with the pain of separation.

Consciousness itself necessitates separation, the division between subject and object. Only in the higher consciousness of the Self is there no duality; there the knower and the knowledge are one. But to reach this quality of consciousness the feminine needs to experience the penetrating power of masculine spirit which appears to violate her instinctual wholeness. This experience of violation is a loss of unconscious oneness, a loss that is necessary if the wayfarer is to reach the higher consciousness of the Self. The instinctual sense of wholeness is broken in order to be reborn in a different dimension.

The masculine path takes the wayfarer away from the illusion of forms into the formless inner reality, from which he returns with a quality of consciousness that can embrace the two worlds. He discovers the oneness beneath the veils of duality. The feminine always embraces this oneness because she is made to carry the sacredness of life within her womb. She is a part of the Great Mother who is the oneness of all life. But that knowledge is hidden within her, and, like all aspects of the Great Mother, carries the taboo of consciousness. The great flow of all life does not know its own oneness. Only humankind has the ability to make this oneness conscious, and yet consciousness carries the pain of separation, the eviction from the paradise of oneness.

In order to consciously know her own oneness, the feminine has to bear the cruelty of consciousness, which can feel like a violation of her own sacred self. She has to learn to contain the contradictions of a world in which her instinctual oneness appears lost. The masculine spirit of consciousness confronts the feminine with duality, but this duality contains the seed of her higher consciousness. The rape of Persephone separates maiden from mother, but also takes us inside the cycles of nature into the mysteries of the soul.

THE DUAL MOVEMENT OF THE SPIRAL

One of the difficulties confronting the contemporary wayfarer is that most texts describing the spiritual journey have been written by men and emphasize the masculine journey of renunciation. They stress the need to turn away from the world and seek a oneness that can only be found elsewhere. The ancient feminine mysteries embrace life and reveal its secret meaning. But these mysteries were rarely written down. In Greece they were taught at Eleusis and for over a thousand years were the center of religious life of antiquity, but it is a testament to their power that despite the thousands of initiates their secrets have never been made known. The feminine is naturally hidden and the secrets of creation do not show themselves easily.

The quality of the masculine is consciousness. While the feminine likes to remain hidden, the masculine seeks to make itself known. The masculine leaves its imprint only too visibly while the feminine is veiled. We live in a culture that values what is visible and easily rejects what is hidden, yet we know we need to embrace both. The masculine and feminine need to be united in our quest, for they are both a part of the spiral path that is our journey Home.

A spiral has both a circular and a linear movement. The masculine is what takes us in a linear direction, towards a goal, which can appear to be upward or downward but in truth is inward. This linear direction demands a focus of intent and a conscious commitment to persevere despite all the difficulties that may be encountered. The feminine is the spiral's circular movement which is inclusive. The feminine requires us to be flexible and continually changing, inwardly responsive to the inner oscillations of the path. To remain fixed is to remain static, caught in a concept or locality. The journey of annihilation is a journey of freedom in which all concepts and ideologies are swept away. We need to allow ourself to change beyond recognition, to be swept into a dance that takes us beyond ourself. The Sufi Master Bhai Sahib described where he lived as "a house of drunkards and a house of change."

Both men and women have masculine and feminine qualities and these are reflected in our spiritual drive. In each of us masculine and feminine are emphasized to a differing degree. There is also the collective conditioning that may overshadow our natural tendencies. For some women the masculine focus of the quest is easier than the all-embracing feminine; the ideal of renunciation is easier than the instinctual awareness of life's sacred nature. This masculine emphasis can be the result of cultural conditioning, a wounding of the feminine, or a deep orientation of the soul. Just as there are many variations across the physical spectrum of masculine and feminine, so is a wayfarer's orientation not limited to sexual typecasting. There are men who are in tune with the creative dance of life and can find the Beloved most easily in the mysterious beauty of His forms. An artist may have this spiritual temperament, and through surrendering to his work come closer to Him whom he loves.

On the spiral dance of death we need to embrace both masculine and feminine qualities, to breathe in and to breathe out. Yet we also need to acknowledge our own nature, to find our own way of being with God. The Sufi Râbi'a was one of the great women saints and she stressed the supremacy of divine love in contrast to some of the earlier Sufis who stressed asceticism. Yet she had a quality of inner focus that could not be disturbed. She could not be distracted by the forms of the world, as in the story of when, one glorious spring day, she was sitting inside with the shutters drawn. Her maid came to open them, saying, "Look outside at the beauty the Creator has made." But she refused to step outside, and Rûmî tells one version of her response:

> The gardens and the fruits are in the heart—
> Only the reflection of His kindness is in
>   this water and clay.[2]

Rûmî himself withdrew from the world when he met Shams-i Tabrîz. Divine love called him and he left his family and disciples, making them so jealous that in the end they chased Shams away. With Shams Rûmî travelled the road that leads far beyond the forms of this world:

> I was invisible awhile, I was dwelling with
> Him.
> I was in the Kingdom of "or nearer," I saw
> what I have seen.
> ... I have gathered a wealth of roses in the
> garden of Eternity,
> I am not of water nor fire, I am not of the
> forward wind,
> I am not of moulded clay: I have mocked
> them all.
> O son, I am not Shams-i Tabrîz, I am the
> pure Light.
> If thou seest me, beware! Tell not anyone
> what thou hast seen![3]

But Rûmî's capacious nature embraced both the masculine and the feminine. In the same poem he also describes a oneness with life in its differing aspects:

> I am the pangs of the jealous, I am the
> pain of the sick.
> I am both cloud and rain: I have rained on
> the meadows.

Unlike Râbi'a, Rûmî celebrates the beauty and wonder of the creation:

> Thanks to the gaze of the sun, the soil
> became a tulip bed—
> To sit at home is now a plague, a plague![4]

To deny the creation is to deny the link of love that runs through all of life. Within the heart there is no separation, no need to turn away from form, because it embraces formlessness. Love is an ocean without limits and the feminine includes everything within her sacred arms.

INCLUSION AND EXCLUSION

Feminine and masculine, inclusion and exclusion—the wayfarer needs both these qualities: the wisdom of union and the wisdom of separation. On the path of love even renunciation is a limitation, as in the saying that "Renunciation of renunciation is renunciation." To be "in the world but not of the world" is to embrace the world with all of its confusions and glory, "the pangs of the jealous, the pain of the sick." When we open our heart to life we are not limited by duality or caught in contradictions. The heart is the home of the Self and the Self contains the opposites within Its essential oneness.

Multiplicity reflects oneness; oneness makes itself known through multiplicity. To deny the wonder of multiplicity is to deny the life that enables us to recognize that He is One. We are not only a mirror to His beauty but a part of His beauty. We carry within ourself the hidden secret of creation, the secret that is brought into existence by the very word of creation, *Kun* ("Be!").

The feminine, caring for all of her children, knows the danger of exclusion. Life is sacred only in its entirety, only because *everything is He*. True renunciation is not the renunciation of the world but the renunciation of the ego. However, because the ego's identity is so embedded in the outer world, in possessions and attachments, turning away from the world can be a process of breaking the grip of the ego, freeing ourself from its patterns of identity. If our individual identity is contained in an outer position, in a beautiful house or in the car we drive, we are imprisoned in these limitations. Struggling to look only towards Truth, to identify with what is highest within ourself, we need to cut these cords of attachment.

In turning away from the world, the wayfarer is turning from the ego towards the Self. The Self, "lesser than the least, greater than the greatest," is a quality of wholeness that contains everything, including all life, within itself. The Self cannot exclude anything, as reflected in the story of the soldier who asked Jâmî if he was a thief. The great saint replied, "What am I not?" Turning towards the Self, the wayfarer's personal self becomes included within the greater dimension of his innermost being: "whole, he passes into the Whole."[5]

Renunciation is a falling away of attachments as the wayfarer is caught and held within the larger dimension of the Self. The lesser falls away under the influence of the greater. Each step we take on the path towards Truth increases the influence of the Self, whose energy has the effect of dissolving patterns of ego attachments. The Self gives the wayfarer the power to turn away from the world. Without this power we would be forever under the spell of the ego and its patterns of illusion. The ego is so strong and its attachments so potent that the wayfarer could never break its grip. Only because we are included within the gravitational pull of the Self are we able to make the transition, step into the spiral of the path.

At the root of renunciation is the Self's totality of inclusion. But this inclusion demands that we leave behind the ego, that we "die before we die." We need to cooperate with the energy of wholeness that separates us from our own identity, our values and attachments. We need to see the limitations of our own life as we know it, its emptiness and illusory nature. To be embraced by the Self is to have to break through the barriers of creation into the dimension of eternity and our essential nonexistence. We need the sword of love to cut us away from our attachments, just as we need the warmth of love to melt the boundaries of our own being.

Contraction and expansion, inbreathing and outbreathing—the path is a continual process of movement and change. There are times when we need to focus and keep our attention one-pointed. But there are also periods of expansion when the heart opens to include a diversity of experiences, when the manifold aspects of both ourself and the Beloved come into consciousness. The real limitation is to remain caught in one stage, in the masculine dynamic of contraction or the feminine quality of expansion. Each has its time and purpose, and then changes into its opposite. The guidance of the Self and the energy of the path activate the movement of the spiral and the inner process that accompanies it. The danger is that we can remain attached to a particular spiritual dynamic. For each of us, different aspects of the path are easier and more appealing. Some wayfarers find the masculine energy of renunciation more attractive, while the feminine work of inclusion may evoke feelings of vulnerability. Others are naturally attuned to the work of embracing, and find the knife of exclusion difficult to wield.

DIFFERENT CHALLENGES FOR MEN AND WOMEN

We all have masculine and feminine qualities within us, but men and women are made differently: physically, psychologically, and spiritually. Because a woman creates new life from her own body she has an instinctual understanding of the spiritual essence of life. This knowledge comes from the creative power of God which she receives in her spiritual and psychic centers at birth. A man has to work hard to gain this knowledge. A man needs to transmute his instinctual power drive until it is surrendered to the will of God. A woman's instinctual nature always connects her with the spiritual essence of life, but man's instinctual drive has to be transformed in order to realize its divine potential. In her natural self, woman is always at the sacred center. A man has to make his heroic journey in order to rediscover within himself his spiritual nature.

Women instinctively know life's wholeness, but find it difficult to leave outer attachments. Generally it is easier for men to be detached and to focus on an invisible goal. Irina Tweedie explains this:

> Because women have children they are made in such a way that things of this world are more important than for a man. We need warmth, we need security. For a woman a home, warmth, security, love, are very much more important than for a man. You will see in India many more male *sannyasins* than female *sannyasins*. For a woman it is much more difficult to renounce the world.... For us women spiritual life is easier than for men, but to renounce is more difficult than for men. [6]

For a woman, detachment can carry the pain of cutting her away from the all-inclusive nature of life. Although the Great Mother embraces everything, she requires that her children remain unconscious and bound to her in servitude. The spiritual path takes us beyond the limits of created nature: we become bound to the Creator and not to His creation. The wayfarer bows down before no one but God. Detachment is the work of freeing oneself from the grip of creation while at the same time honoring its sacred nature.

The alchemists called the process of transformation an *opus contra naturam* because they understood how the enclosed cycle of nature must be broken for a higher level of consciousness to evolve. Consciousness involves separation, and while the feminine honors the wholeness of life she also needs to break free from a total dependence upon the Great Mother. The symbol of ouroboros, the serpent eating its tail, images the realm of the Great Mother in which everything returns upon itself, and the wheel of life keeps us endlessly imprisoned.

A boy's passage into manhood instinctually frees him from the mother. His spiritual journey is then to rediscover this sacred wholeness within himself. The girl never leaves the arms of the Great Mother, and womanhood is a celebration of her belonging to the creative cycle. A girl's first menstruation symbolizes how she holds the power of creation within her body and can herself become mother. Learning to become detached can feel like a violation of life's all-embracing nature, and can also carry the guilt that comes with freedom and higher consciousness.

Guilt is a weapon that the Great Mother wields with great effectiveness in order to keep her children imprisoned. Women, being closer to the Great Mother, are more susceptible to the effects of guilt. For example, a woman who was on retreat became aware that although she loved her husband and children, she was also quite happy alone. This revelation surprised her with a new-found inner freedom, but she quickly felt guilty: "Maybe it is wrong to feel happy being alone when I am a mother and wife." Through such feelings of guilt the Great Mother works to draw her daughter back into the womb of the collective where she belongs just as mother and wife. The woman at the retreat needed to be reassured of the importance of the new consciousness awakening within her, and that it was in no way contradictory to her maternal role.

The spiritual journey is a work of bringing into consciousness our own inner connection to the Beloved. Every soul carries the imprint of His face, the memory of His nearness. Bringing the heart's remembrance into daily life means to consciously acknowledge our spiritual dimension. While women are more instinctively attuned to the sacred, consciousness is a masculine quality. The nature of the feminine is to remain hidden and veiled, and the Great Mother has placed a great taboo upon consciousness. To make conscious the mystery of life's sacred essence can feel like a violation of Her command to keep this secret hidden.

Consciousness also carries the pain of limitation. The nature of the unconscious is unlimited and undefined. The ocean of the unconscious is without borders or differentiation. The moment something is made conscious it is defined and limited by this definition. To say something is "like this" excludes it from being otherwise. This is against the all-inclusive nature of the feminine. The feminine also knows the danger of definition, how easily life can become crystallized and lose its dynamic, evolutionary nature. The essence of life cannot be fixed or limited, and in the very process of naming what is sacred its eternal nature can be lost. The ancient wisdom of the Tao expresses this:

> The tao that can be told
> is not the eternal Tao.
> The name that can be named
> is not the Eternal name.
> The unnameable is the eternally real.
> Naming is the origin
> of all particular things.
>
> Free from desire, you realize the mystery.
> Caught in desire, you see only the
>   manifestations.
>
> Yet mystery and manifestations
> arise from the same source.
> This source is called darkness.
>
> Darkness within darkness.
> The gateway to all understanding.[7]

The feminine knows the mystery and instinctually feels the peril of making this mystery conscious. What the heart knows cannot be understood with the mind. Yet the spiritual path involves the work of bringing together the inner and outer worlds, living outwardly in harmony with one's innermost self. Keeping one's feet upon a path which is "as narrow as the edge of a razor" needs the light of conscious discrimination. We need to see the path as clearly as we are able. Ultimately the wayfarer knows that he cannot know, as in the prayer of Abû Bakr: "Praise to God who hath given His creatures no way of attaining to the knowledge of Him except through their inability to know Him."[8] But in order to live in this world as His servant, constantly attentive to His will, we need to know in the mind as well as in the heart that we belong to Him.

The feminine, attuned to the mystery of what is hidden, can experience consciousness as a cruel and bleak light that brings limitation and misunderstanding. The sacred can seem violated by a harshness that denies both subtlety and change. There is a further difficulty in that the consciousness of our contemporary world is dominated by rationalism and materialism. As a result we lack even the language to describe the qualities of the spiritual. Our language has developed to describe a rational view of a tangible outer reality, and the poverty of language to articulate feelings is an example of our difficulty in describing a fluid, irrational, inner experience. The inner world and its experiences lack the clear divisions which characterize the outer world. A similar limitation of verbal language has become evident in describing recent subatomic field theories, where

> ...the task of articulation requires that a vision of a dynamic, mutually interacting field be represented through a medium that is inherently linear, fragmented and unidirectional.[9]

Making the spiritual conscious confronts the wayfarer with a collective culture, its language and thought-forms, that have for centuries rejected the sacred in favor of the rational and the material. The limitations of consciousness have never been more evident.

One further difficulty confronting women in our western culture is the way its masculine values in themselves can be experienced as a violation of the feminine. Entering the patriarchal workplace, women are often forced to adopt masculine attitudes and goals that violate their instinctual awareness of the sacred wholeness of life. In order to compete or just survive in today's world a woman may have had to sacrifice her nurturing, maternal self. The emptiness that many people feel in today's material culture can be traced to the fact that the feminine's role of carrying the sacred meaning of life has been rejected and forgotten. The quality of joy that belongs to life lived from a sacred center has been replaced by a search for pleasure. We all suffer from this collective impoverishment, but women, being closer to the core of creation, feel this desolation and violation more strongly. Yet for the same reason more women than men are at the present time attracted to spiritual life. Women feel more acutely the need within themselves and within the collective to remedy this primal pain. But at the same time there is an understandable fear that the mystery which they bring from the soul into consciousness will be again abused and rejected.

A man needs to rediscover what has been lost to masculine consciousness, learn to surrender his in-stinctual power drive so that the feminine soul can give birth to the divine mystery. He has to cross the threshold of vulnerability and lay down his sword at the feet of his inner feminine. A woman carries the divine essence in every cell of her body, in the very substance of herself. She needs to bring this sacred self into consciousness despite the fear of violation and pain of misunderstanding. Freeing herself from her attachments in this world, she is able to consciously know and nourish others with the mystery that forms the fabric of her being:

.Free from desire, you realize the mystery.
Caught in desire, you see only the
manifestations.

THE CIRCLE OF THE SELF

While the arms of the Great Mother embrace all of creation, the circle of the Self includes the two worlds. Renunciation is not a denial of life but an affirmation of the soul's freedom. Consciously acknowledging our spiritual nature, we step off the endless cycle of life and death onto the spiral path that leads to the very center where non-being and being meet. Here, where creation is born out of nothingness, love comes into the world and life is imprinted with its deepest purpose.

The wayfarer's *conscious* commitment to his or her spiritual self is the key that opens the door to this path beyond creation. Locked within the ego we see only the horizons of time and space. When we affirm the Self we begin the work of limiting the ego's autonomy. This work of limitation is a period of constriction that is painful and demanding. But it is mirrored by an inner expansion as the dimension of the Self opens within us. This inner expansion is not immediately accessible to consciousness. We need to develop a new organ of consciousness in order to experience the inner dimension that is being revealed. The eye of the heart has to open.

We need perseverance if we are to stay on the path as the experience of limitation intensifies. We need to remain focused on our invisible goal despite the difficulties placed in our way by the dying ego. As the ego's horizon closes in we have to trust that we are being guided and not deceived. This period of transition usually lasts for several years, although it will vary in intensity. The opening of the eye of the heart takes time and requires patience.

Gradually we make the transition from the ego to the Self. Within the Self the masculine and feminine aspects of the journey merge together, and there also any distinction ceases between the wayfarer and the path: "Since in Unity there is no distinction, the Quest and the Way and the Seeker become one."[10] The journey to God becomes the journey in God as the servant comes under the direct influence of his Lord. There are still times of expansion and times of contraction, but they are experienced directly within the heart and come from the Beloved. When aspects of His beauty are revealed, the heart opens and experiences His kindness, His mercy, and His grace. Then there are times when His majesty is revealed, namely power, magnificence, and might. Then the servant is absorbed in awe. Finally contraction and expansion happen simultaneously as Najm al-Dîn Kubrâ describes:

> In the first stage of entering this arena the heart is at times expanded...and at times contracted.... This is however the stage of variegation in the arena of contraction and expansion. But the one who has been established in it is contracted-expanded [synchronically]...they are contracted in their bodies as if fettered by chains

from the intensity of veneration (*waqâr*), perseverance (*anâh*), and remembrance (*tidskâr*), and [at the same time they are] expanded in their hearts and spirits like the expansion of a fine skin when the winds blow.[11]

The servant bows down before his Lord at the same time as his heart expands from the presence of his Beloved.

When the ego is surrendered, we step into the all-embracing arena of the Self. The Self allows the ego the autonomy it needs in order to function in everyday life. The wayfarer needs to keep constant vigilance as the ego may try to overstep its boundaries and increase its power. We need to keep an inner eye always watching that the ego not make new attachments, that we remain free. Constantly vigilant, we know that the ego waits behind every corner, subtly trying to seduce us back into the illusions of the world. Sometimes the ego can become frightened by a deepening awareness of the infinite inner emptiness, and try to pull us back from this brink. But once we are surrendered we are protected and guided by the energy of the Self. Spiritual evolution does not go backwards.

On the Sufi path the wayfarer is protected not just by the Self but by the chain of transmission that holds us in the grace of the tradition. The heart of the wayfarer is held within the heart of the teacher, and when we are surrendered this merging of love protects us with both power and grace. When Irina Tweedie was with her teacher, Bhai Sahib, she noticed the deep fondness he had towards his grandson, and was concerned that he might be attached. But he responded:

Those who are always with their Guru do not
possess worldly things. They rest in their Guru,
and everything else does not touch them. I am
merged in my Rev. Guru Maharaj. All else is
here; I partake of it....[12]

Although we live in the world we are immersed
elsewhere. The world falls from us and we remain
unattached: "If you go and have a bath in the Ganga,·
and you go out, does it remain with you?—of course
not!"[13]

NO BIRD AND NO WING

Surrendered to the Self, the wayfarer is in a state of
both total inclusion and total renunciation. Everything
within the two worlds is held within the circle of the
Self, a circle "whose center is everywhere and circum-
ference nowhere." The Self is free from any limitation,
any attachment. Free even from the need for renunciation, the lover looks only to the Beloved. This is the
state of mystical poverty, the poverty of the heart,
whose "inner truth is that the servant is independent of
all except God."[14] Mystical poverty is the heart's inner
attachment to its Beloved and freedom from all other
attachments. It is in this sense that the Sufi regards
absolute poverty as absolute richness.

Mystical poverty allows the lover to know his
Beloved in the inner and outer worlds. Attached to the
world of forms, we see only the outer shape of
creation. Unattached to forms, the eye of the heart sees
the secret hidden in the outer world, the feminine
mystery of creation that came into being with the
command "*Kun!*" In the words of 'Attâr,

If the eye of the heart is open
In each atom there will be one hundred
secrets.[15]

The Sufi poet Shûshtarî describes how the state of
poverty draws the lover into the inner mystery of his
own being, where he is able to make the true connection between the outer and inner world, and thus
realize creation's secret:

> If my clay veils me
>   from my essence,
> the richness of my poverty
>   draws me to me.
> You who seek poverty,
>   if you connect
> the corporeal world
>   with the Secret,
> creation and its mandate,
> the Name will be revealed to you at once.
> You will see the extent
>   of the command—*kun!*—
> and He Who is its Initiator.[16]

Poverty is an inner emptiness which reveals the
Name hidden at the core of creation. Within the heart,
poverty is a state of annihilation in which there is only
the oneness of love. Love's oneness is symbolized by
the first letter of the Arabic alphabet, ١ (*alif*), which
"represents graphically the straightness, non-deviation
and unity of all opposites within the source and
beginning of phenomena."[17] This oneness which is
both the beginning and the end of creation is eternally
present within every atom. For the lover this one letter,
Alif, is written in fire on the back of the heart. Within

the heart His oneness burns away the veils of duality. Externally the lover may remain in the world of multiplicity, but his love for God has merged into God's love for him. Kubrâ explains this state in which the opposites have been united and then dissolved:

> When the lover is annihilated in Love his love becomes one with the Love of the Beloved, and then there is no bird and no wing, and his flight and love to God are by God's Love to him, and not to Him by him.[18]

As we travel the path of love, the opposites spiral inward towards the center where the two worlds meet. What we know as ourselves, the form of the lover, remains in the outer world of opposites. We feel the fluctuations of the heart, the expansions and contractions of love. But inwardly the states of the lover, the stages of the journey, have been replaced by the effects of the Beloved, "who holds the heart of the faithful between two of His fingers and turns it as He wills." The masculine and feminine aspects of the path are merged into oneness as "The mystic passes away from what belongs to himself and persists through what belongs to God, while conversely he persists through what belongs to God, and so passes away from what belongs to himself...."[19]

OBEDIENCE AND FREEDOM

Forget your figuring. Forget your self. Listen to your Friend.
When you become totally obedient to that one,
you'll be free.

Rûmî[1]

THE HONOR OF SERVANTHOOD

The paradoxes of the Self arise into consciousness from deep in the inner world. Dreams, not being limited by the constrictions of the rational mind, can embrace the opposites and open us to their mysterious union.

A young boy aged ten to twelve appears on a horse. He is of noble birth and stature—a chevalier. He is nobly dressed, wearing a distinctive hat looking like a bishop's mitre. On the outside of the hat is a golden lace brocade covering a deep red, luminous material. The horse, too, is noble and well fitted out.

The boy's function is to deliver the king's messages throughout the land. He is related to the king or one of his ministers. As the emissary of the king he is greatly respected. He has carried out this function for generations, and so is well known throughout the land. But he never grows old.

He is summoned to the Royal Court and

117

given a sealed document which is the death
sentence for a young girl at the far end of the
kingdom. As he rides off with the document he
finds himself bending over with its weight. As he
continues, even the horse staggers and has to
brace itself because of the weight of this document. Because of this weight it takes several
years for him to reach his destination.

As he arrives at the court of justice and/or
prison, he abandons his usual custom of not
standing upon ceremony and acting with dispatch on the king's authority. Instead, he kneels
at the foot of the High Justice, removes his hat
for the very first time, and places in it the
dispatch. Raising the hat above his head he
presents it to the High Justice. As the Justice
removes the dispatch a transformation occurs.
The death sentence turns into a grant of clem-
ency and freedom to the young girl, who during
the years of the young man's journey has blos-
somed into a beautiful young woman. At the
same time the hat changes into a beggar's bowl,
and the boy is transformed into an old man in
beggar's clothes who immediately leaves the
court to become a beggar on the street. From
that very moment he is recognized as a familiar
figure to all who encounter him, as though he
has always been there.

Throughout the years of his begging he
approaches every family in the land. Only when
this is done, and he has been given their charity,
can he travel to the end of the land where he
comes to a plateau overlooking the kingdom.
He now has no further use for the begging bowl,

but continues to keep it because it carries traces and smells of all the charities he has received.

On the plateau, on its edge, he sits in meditation with the bowl covering his heart. He overlooks the kingdom.

This dream told by a man recounts a story so ancient and archetypal that it resonates with the mystery of the soul. Who is to be condemned and who is liberated? Who is the king and who is the judge? Who is the courtier and who is the beggar?

As the emissary of the king the dreamer reflects the grandeur of his master. His splendid hat, his magnificent horse, and the respect he is given belong to his position as servant. Carrying the orders of the king, he is treated in accordance with the status of the king. His unfailing obedience is his worth. Obedience is the mark of the servant of God, who aspires that His will be done. Surrender to the will of God is one of the first steps of the wayfarer, turning away from the ego towards the Self.

Seeking always to please our Beloved, we listen to the guidance that comes from within, trying to distinguish between the voice of the ego and the voice of the Self, the hint from God within the heart. Discrimination is one of the most difficult spiritual virtues; it is only learned through mistakes. How do we know that we are really following the guidance of the Self and not the deceptive voice of the ego? One of the first indications is whether we have anything personally to gain from this "guidance." The ego is only concerned with its own self-interest, while the Self follows His will. Yet there are no definite rules for discrimination, for, as in the story of Khidr and Moses, the ways of God follow a different path from those of the ego and the mind. Moses, despite his good intentions, could not stay with Khidr who unconditionally acted according to higher laws.[2] As in many aspects of the mystical path, true discrimination is born from the wayfarer's inner attitude, his ability to be attuned to a quality of knowing that is beyond the rational mind.

The dreamer, as the emissary of the king, is highly respected. When we follow the will of the Self, a subtle change happens as the aspects of the psyche acknowledge our relationship to the Self. An inner dignity develops that comes from the pride of the Self, the true nobility of the human being. The code of honor that belonged to warriors, knights, and gentlemen was an outer manifestation of this quality of pride that is very different from the pride of the ego. The true knight was someone who was trained according to ancient spiritual principles, and as the Grail legends portray, was in service to the divine feminine, Our Lady. Sadly our secular society has lost touch with the real meaning of honor, and only too often the "honor" of the ego replaces the deeper honor of the Self. The pride of the Self belongs to service; the dignity of the servant is only a reflection of his Lord.

Following His will, we are aligned with our real dignity. We learn to walk with our head held high in a world that has forgotten Him. The western collective attitude that the world belongs to mankind and not to God is an example of the arrogance of a culture that is dominated by ego-consciousness. Furthermore, if the ego, the individual self, is seen as the sole center of consciousness, servanthood can only mean subservience to another's will or the patterns of the collective. Recognizing what is higher than the ego, we need to reclaim the sacred nature of service and the inner honor it brings. We need to bring into consciousness the spiritual relationship of the ego to the Self and the Self to God. In the Grail legends, which embody a western spiritual tradition, the knight searches for the Holy Grail, a symbol of the spiritual center of man and the universe. When the knight finds the Grail, but before he can claim this treasure, he needs to ask the question, "Whom serves the Grail?" To which the answer is given, "The Grail serves the Grail King." If the knight does not ask this question, the Grail and the Grail castle vanish and his quest has to begin again. Asking the question is to make conscious the connection of service that is at the core of spiritual life.

Sufis are known as His servants, and one of their titles for their Beloved is "the servant of His servants." For the Sufi the role of servanthood has it origins at the primordial covenant when God asked the not-yet-created humanity, "Am I not your Lord?" Humanity's response, "Yes, we witness it," is reflected in the primal duty of the servant which is to acknowledge that He is Lord. The saying of the Prophet, "I am the servant of 'There is no god but God,'"[3] reflects the work of the wayfarer to bring into consciousness humanity's pledge to witness Him as Lord.

The servant belongs to his Master since before the beginning of time. When we recognize our role as servant we bring this knowledge of the soul into the dimension of time and space, and are honored by the possibility of serving Him. We bring the remembrance of the heart into consciousness and into life. The difference between sacred servanthood and an ego-dominated life depends not upon outer action but inner attitude. The ego can easily delude us that we are

121

"helping others," or "doing God's work," when we are in fact feeding patterns of co-dependency or inflation. The role of servant is an inner attitude of attention to our Lord.

THE ATTENTION OF THE HEART

Remembering our role as servant is an inner alignment with the Self that frees us from the ego's domination. The act of recognition that He is Lord is a fundamental and powerful statement to both our self and our environment. Only when we have imprinted into the psyche and consciousness our role as servant can we freely follow His will.

But because our culture values "doing" above "being," we may think that spiritual service necessitates "good deeds." "Being" precedes and is deeper than action, and the foundation of sacred service is "to be here for Him." In our ordinary lives, working, bringing up a family, His servant may live outwardly undistinguished from those who are just following their ego. But inwardly we look to our Lord and are freely bound in service to Him. Keeping our inner connection to Him whom we love is the deepest service we can undertake.

This state of attention belongs both to the mind and to the heart. But while the mind is easily occupied with the outer world, the heart of the devotee is always turned towards God. Service is an attitude of devotion born out of love. We are fulfilled in serving Him whom we love. Love carries the seeds of our devotion into our outer life and actions. Mother Teresa describes the simple truth that it is love that gives substance to our acts of service:

Small things with great love. It is not what we
do but the love we put in the doing, for then we
give it to God and He makes it infinite.

Only He whom we love can give value to our actions,
and through love our acts are taken into His presence.
Only when we keep open the heart's connection does
His touch imprint Itself upon our life, influencing not
only ourself but our surroundings. Through the heart
of His lover He comes into His world.

We affirm with our attitude and actions the soul's
pledge, and so reconnect the two worlds. Servanthood
manifests the inner connection of lover and Beloved,
through which the heart's remembrance and His companionship give joy and meaning to life:

Everyone, standing or sitting,
from the earth to the farthest stars,
Through servanthood to God,
enjoys remembrance and communion.[4]

SACRIFICE

The dream of the king's emissary contains the theme of
sacrifice. The dreamer has to deliver the death sentence for a girl. Who is the girl who is to be sentenced
to death? All the figures in a dream are aspects of the
dreamer's psyche. In a man's psyche a girl is the inner
feminine not yet mature. The inner feminine, which
Jung termed the anima, carries the image of a man's
soul, his hidden self.[5]

What does it mean that the dreamer carries her
death sentence, and why would the king condemn her?

123

When the anima is projected onto the outer world, a man is taken into the magic and suffering of romantic love, into the dreams of desire and the hunt for perfection in another. The anima draws a man into the fascinating world of the feminine, veiling herself in the guise of feminine beauty and mystery. But the lover of God is destined to serve only one Beloved, for, in the words of al-Hallâj, "When Truth has taken hold of a heart She empties it of all but Herself."⁶ The king's death sentence is love's covenant, "You can only love Me. You will find perfection only in Me."

The emissary does not deviate from carrying the king's orders. But this sentence is so heavy that it weighs down upon the rider and his horse, taking him years to deliver the king's command. To accept that fulfillment and love can only come from an invisible Beloved is a heavy load, particularly when we live in a culture that promotes romantic love. We are continually bombarded by songs, films, and other images that describe love, passion, and fulfillment found in an external relationship. Because our culture has forgotten the sacred inner world, the only mystery easily accessible is a human love affair. But His lover is pledged before the beginning of time, and has to honor this commitment, has to deliver this death sentence.

Slowly we walk the road that seems to destroy what is most precious. Saint Augustine prayed, "Give me chastity, Lord. Give me continence.... But not yet!"⁷ The same theme is echoed within many of us. In our heart of hearts we know that we belong to Another, and yet at the same time we are resistant to leaving behind the collective fantasy. We look to find His face in a human lover whom we can touch and hold. We are reluctant to accept that the outer world can never answer our need. A young woman had a dream in which she was looking at a vase of flowers and wanted to know the nature of her love. The flowers turned black and then white. Black is the color of mystical poverty, of being annihilated in God,while white is the color of purity.[8] When we discussed the dream, I told her its symbolism, that the nature of her loving was emptiness, the annihilation of her own self. Her love would be purified, turned white, by being immersed in nothingness. With tearful eyes she asked, "What about relationships?" But the dream stated unequivocally that her loving was only for Him. The emptiness that she felt in her daily life was to be embraced as a lover's touch.

The ancient path of the mystic that leads to the "dark silence in which all lovers lose themselves" is a terrifying commitment. At the beginning our feet are heavy because we sense only the desolation. But once we have passed through the door of non-being we are open to experience the total bliss and tenderness that can only come from the void, from the nothingness of real love. Without the boundaries of form or the limitations of identity we can be immersed in the infinite emptiness of His presence.

DEATH AND FREEDOM

The dreamer follows the orders of the king, carrying the girl's death sentence to the High Justice. On his journey the years have passed and the girl has grown and flowered into a beautiful woman. Our obedience to the king creates a space for inner development in which the soul grows and flowers. Inner obedience to the Self enables Its energy to create a shrine of protection. This shrine is the meeting place of the two worlds.

The inner feminine has matured, developed in beauty and grace. Commitment to the path reveals the wonder of our true being, and also attracts to the psyche higher energies of divine beauty and majesty. But even this must be sacrificed. The death sentence makes the imperative statement that this must be in service to the king. It is a spiritual law that we are never given for ourselves, only for others. The symbolism of sacrifice is to acknowledge that everything belongs to Him and is a part of His higher purpose.

The archetypal story of sacrifice is told in Genesis, when Abraham is made to offer up Isaac, his firstborn. The sacrifice of Isaac embodies the principle that "what is most precious to us must go." But in this story, when Abraham's knife is drawn to slay his son lying on the altar, the angel stops him at the final moment. The real sacrifice is the act of consciously placing ourself and what we value in the hands of God, who is the Lord of life and death. When this sacrifice has been made we are free from the grip of the ego, and death is turned into life. Abraham then sacrifices a ram, a symbolic offering, because the real sacrifice has been made within.

In the dream, when the letter containing the death sentence is delivered, the king's command has changed. The woman is free. Up to now she has been imprisoned, for the mystic knows that the ego and the illusions of this world are an imprisonment. Only when we are surrendered to the Self, obedient to its higher dictates, are we free. In Rûmî's words, "Listen to your Friend. When you become totally obedient to that one, you'll be free." Real freedom embraces the paradox that "only the bondsmen are free," and the deeper paradox of the union of death and life. The girl who had been caught within the limited horizon of ego-consciousness is now a beautiful woman, free to live in the openness of the Self, in service to her own divinity. The soul can now fulfill its deeper destiny in relationship to God, rather than being lived out through projection and caught in the ego's desires.

The real beauty of the feminine is the way she contains and reflects the beauty of the Absolute. The divine feminine *is* a state of surrender to God through which His wonder can be experienced. His lovers who have given themselves to love's deepest desolation come to know this secret of surrender. We gladly become a captive of the mystery that is hidden behind her face:

> If you ask of me the long story
> Of the Beloved's curl,
> I cannot answer, for it contains a mystery
> Which only true lovers understand,
> And they, maddened by its beauty,
> Are held captive as by a golden chain.[9]

POVERTY[10]

The dream's next image is one of transformation: the magnificent hat of the king's emissary becomes a begging bowl, and the boy an old man in beggar's rags. Poverty is the true possession of the Sufi, for it means a state of inner emptiness in which we are nourished by God alone. Our only value is what is given by Him. Having given away both the world and ourself for Him, we stand naked and alone, clothed in the garment of poverty. Ultimately, poverty is a state of annihilation, *fanâ*, in which "the mystic is so totally absorbed in God that he has no longer any existence of his own, neither inwardly nor outwardly, in this world and beyond."[11] Poverty is the total abnegation of the self and the affirmation of the One.

The dreamer's total obedience to the king has transformed him from emissary to beggar. His hat has become his begging bowl. He has changed from a boy, a figure of innocence, into an old man, a figure of wisdom. To walk the streets as a beggar is to carry the wisdom of inner emptiness into daily life. The death sentence, the sacrifice, has emptied him of himself. This state of emptiness will take him into the realm of non-being, the real Home of the mystic. Obedience to the king depends upon the existence of the emissary. But once the dreamer's identity has been lost, sacrificed to love, there is no Lord and no servant. Within the heart there is only His presence or His absence.

"Everything has to go." Every identity must be lost on the journey of love. The work of obedience brings the wayfarer close to his Lord. The image of service stamps into our heart the real relationship of the creation to the Creator. Outwardly we will always remain His servant, but inwardly the heart dissolves, the distinctions of duality are worn away. Emptiness replaces substance. In *The Conference of the Birds* 'Attâr describes the seventh and final valley of the quest as "the Valley of Poverty and Nothingness," in which "The thousand shadows that surround you disappear in a single ray of the celestial sun." Poverty takes us beyond our existence into His existence, in which the paradox of non-being and being reveals itself:

"An impure object dropped into rose-water remains impure because of its innate qualities; but a pure object dropped in the ocean will lose its specific existence and will participate in the ocean and its movements. In ceasing to exist separately it retains its beauty. It exists and non-exists. How can this be? The mind cannot conceive it."[12]

Obedience to the king, and the sacrifice this involves, purify the wayfarer. Our conscious relationship with God is the most powerful agent of inner purification. The greater the light the greater the shadow. In His light even the darkest corners of our shadow become visible as our impurities confront us. Then through His love we can accept and transform our own darkness. There are aspects of our psyche and of the collective psyche that we cannot confront alone, for they would overwhelm us, drag us into the depths. But His light disarms even our most powerful inner demons. The wayfarer is protected by the power of his commitment to the path, by the potency of remembrance (the *dhikr*), and by His companionship (either directly or through the being of the sheikh).

Through our devotion we draw near to Him, like the moth drawn to the flame of love. The fire purifies us, allowing us into His presence where there is no separation, where lover and Beloved are one. The garments of poverty are the clothing for this journey. The begging bowl is an emptiness of intention. Poverty replaces obedience, for how can we be obedient when we have no separate will? Meister Eckhart describes this ultimate state of poverty:

A man must become truly poor and free from his creaturely will as he was when he was born. And I tell you, by the Eternal Truth, that so long as you desire to fulfill the will of God and have any hankering after eternity, for just so long you are not truly poor. He alone has spiritual poverty who *wills nothing, knows nothing, desires nothing*.[13]

Total emptiness of intention allows us to be totally in His hands, to be used as He wills. Our service to the Beloved is this state of emptiness, which is the nearest to union that can exist in this world of separation. As a beggar we walk the streets of the world, no longer depending upon our own will or effort. This state of dependence can be frightening at first, but in the end it offers great security. With an empty bowl we wait for the nourishment we need.

When I started lecturing in Germany I was thrown into such a state of dependence. My teacher had lectured a lot in Germany and so many people came to my lecture and workshop. In America I had become used to doing dreamwork with an audience of sixty to seventy people, but now I found that I had two hundred and fifty people for dreamwork! Normally group dreamwork requires a feeling of intimacy, but here I was in a large seminar room with a microphone on each side of the audience. Those wishing to share a dream lined up behind the microphone. There would be a line of ten people behind each microphone, and more people were waiting to tell their dreams.

Usually in a dreamwork session, when a dream is told, I sometimes have an inspiration, but often I open the dream for group discussion. Different interpretations and associations are offered to the dreamer, who is able to feel which one(s) give insight into the dream. The group participation is powerful and productive, and I do not have the pressure of always having to offer an interpretation. But this situation in Germany was quite different. An audience of two hundred and fifty is just too large for group discussion. Also, with so many people waiting to share their dream there was not the time. The situation was further complicated by the fact that I do not speak German, and so the whole proceeding went via an interpreter sitting next to me. Normally when someone tells a dream I listen very carefully to the dream as it comes from the unconscious of the dreamer. The feeling in the words often carries different levels of meaning. But in this case I could not directly understand what the dreamer was saying and a translation does not carry the feeling quality.

All of my usual dream-interpretation techniques had to be left behind. There was little time to work with the dreamer on detailed associations. It was inappropriate to open the dream to group discussion and I often missed the subtleties of feeling in the words. There was also the pressure and expectation of the dreamer and all the people waiting to tell their dream. My only resource was to pray. Listening to the dream I would be as empty as possible and in the emptiness offer myself. I could not be dependent upon my own ability, only upon His guidance.

It worked. Intimacy and energy were present in the room. People shared their dreams and were given the response they needed. At the end of the week-end I was left exhausted but in awe. Like a tap that is turned on and then turned off I had been used. I had experienced the effectiveness of being totally dependent upon Him. The situation had forced me into a state of poverty.

WATCHING THE WORLD

The saying, "When poverty becomes perfect (complete), it is God,"[14] describes the fact that when we are totally dependent upon Him we invoke His presence. Just as nature does not allow a vacuum, our state of emptiness is filled by Him. I had experienced this in a crowded lecture room. The dreamer's empty bowl would also be filled as he travelled the king's land, no longer emissary but beggar. When his journey is finished even the begging bowl is no longer needed. Dependence upon God changes into a state of merging. With the empty bowl covering his heart, which is the place of merging, the dreamer is in meditation, overlooking the kingdom. Inwardly united with his Beloved, he watches over His world.

Through our obedience we come near to Him, freeing ourself of ourself. Then, when all of our patterns of resistance, even our very desire for existence, have been sacrificed, we can fulfill the deepest function of servanthood, to be His eyes and ears:

> My servant ceases not to draw nigh unto Me
> by works of devotion, until I love him, and when
> I love him I am the eye by which he sees and the
> ear by which he hears.[15]

As His eyes and ears, the wayfarer has a dual function. Looking through the wayfarer, the Creator is able to take care of His world. It is for this reason that it is said that wherever there is trouble in the world a Sufi is there, helping. Unattached to the conditioning of the outer world, we are able to bring His attention to the real need of a situation. But our deepest service to the Beloved is as a vehicle through which He can come to know Himself. "I was a Hidden Treasure. I longed to be known so I created the world." Through the empty eye of His servant He can see His reflection in His world. The Creator can come to know Himself in His creation.

MERGING WITH THE TEACHER

The dream of the emissary and the beggar describes a mystery of spiritual transformation, how the stages of the path evolve within a human being. It is a lifetime's journey to take up the bowl of poverty and learn to live free from the dominance of the ego. How does it happen? How is the wayfarer changed so that emptiness can reveal its secret? Is a firmness of intention enough, or do we need a ferryman to help us cross to the shore of non-being?

The Sufi says that you need a teacher to make this journey, to make the lover spin with the speed of emptiness. We stand on the shore, excited at the prospect of the journey, encouraged by travellers' tales. But how can we leave our self behind? Rûmî simply states that it cannot be done alone:

> If you want dervishood, spiritual poverty,
> and emptiness, you must be Friends with a Sheikh.
> Talking about it, reading books, and doing practices
> don't help. Soul receives from soul that Knowing.
>
> The mystery of spiritual opening may be living
> in a pilgrim's heart, and yet the knowing of it
> may not yet be his.

Wait for the illuminating openness,
as though your chest were filling with Light,
as when God said,

> *Did We not expand you?*
>
> (Qur'an XCIV,1)[16]

There is a secret way the soul opens to God that belongs to the masters of the tradition, to those who have been made empty and infused with the knowledge of opening others. Sufism is a living tradition, and this wisdom is not stored in books. When the disciple is ready the teacher is there, waiting to awaken the innermost center. As with Rûmî, our Shams waylays us and performs his work, breaking down the barriers of the ego and whirling us into the emptiness of our true being. From heart to heart the transmission of love takes place.

At different stages of the journey different qualities of consciousness are awakened, for the heart's illumination is not a single happening. Consciousness expands gradually as we are drawn further and further into the limitless ocean of love. The difficulties of the journey prepare us for each experience of expansion, but these moments are always a gift, an act of grace. In one instant the king changes the death sentence to freedom, and robes of poverty appear.

Such changes take place on the inner planes, on the level of the soul. They are beyond the level of the mind, but are reflected into consciousness. The mind grasps the experience according to its limitations. In a dream we may be given a glimpse of our own unfolding and the way the teacher transforms us. The following dream-experience is one friend's wonder, but it images an opening into oneness that happens to every wayfarer:

I go to visit my teacher. We meditate together and then welcome each other with love and joy. He looks into my eyes and his eyes are shining like diamonds. Then he takes me into his arms and begins to dance with me. Wonderful music is playing and we turn around like a couple accustomed to dancing with each other. When I realize that we are really dancing I become slightly cramped, but he tells me to relax and I let myself fall into the turning.

In the meantime the music finishes and we are the music. We are dancing *The Song of the Superior.* Suddenly it happens, unexpectedly— the teacher and I and our movements become united—we melt together. He becomes me and I become him. In that moment I realize and feel how everything is turning, really turning—it is turning around the center of God. I have been catapulted into the universe and see how the whole universe is turning around God in the time of the swinging—everything that has been created, galaxies, stars, suns, moons, atoms, stones, water, microbes, wood, yes, each and all in the human being—everything and all is turning around God; all is just one harmony, all is dancing His song, all life and all the universe together. I am All and Everything—for a short moment united with Him.

Then I realize that I am dancing with my teacher and we have finished dancing the circle. He smiles and says to me, "Next time you will be leading." And I know that I was only able to have this experience because my feet permanently touch the ground.

The dance with the teacher takes us from duality to oneness. We dance the ancient song of the spiritual tradition, the lineage of the friends of God who are the path. Our superiors walk before us, and from heart to heart the oneness of love is passed down, the transmission of fire. The heart of the sheikh is merged into the heart of his sheikh which is merged into God. Without this lineage of love we would remain stranded in duality. When we are embraced by the essence of the teacher we are embraced by oneness.

First the dreamer relaxes into the music and the dance. Then the music ceases and the dancers become the music and the dance is *The Song of the Superior.* They dance the timeless turning of teacher and disciple, soul in harmony with soul. Then "suddenly it happened, unexpectedly," as two unite into one. Merging with the teacher is one of the central mysteries of the Sufi path. This merging of souls cannot be understood by the mind, but it is a real, inner happening. It lifts the dreamer out of the ego into the Self where he sees how "everything is turning around the center of God." Every atom belongs to God and dances in praise around Him. Rûmî, experiencing this mystical truth, taught his dervishes to whirl, mirroring the whirling universe:

> For when you enter in the dance
> >   you leave both these worlds
> For outside these two worlds there lies
> >   the universe, endless, of whirling.
> ...Whatever there is, is only He,
> >   your foot steps there in dancing:
> The whirling, see, belongs to you,
> >   and you belong to the whirling.[17]

In this dance we "leave both these worlds," for we are merged into the oneness that is their center and source. We become the center and the dancing universe. There is no duality, only the turning of love.

For an instant the dreamer experiences mystical union: "I am All and everything—for a short moment united with Him." Merging with the teacher is the stepping stone to merging with God. Union is born from union. Through the inner connection with the sheikh, the grace of the Beloved imprints the heart with a glimpse of the "Oneness of Being." The real unity of life is revealed as a living, dynamic dance. The dreamer is a part of this dance which is "His Song."

Once we know how the creation circles the Creator and is bound by ties of union, we are always in service. This service comes from the heart, from the center of our own being where He is present. He is in service to Himself. The dreamer witnesses this relationship, for he has seen how all of creation sings His song. He has experienced the unity within multiplicity, that there is only one song and the whole of life is that song. He performs the deepest service of love, witnessing the oneness of the Beloved. He knows that "Wheresoever you turn there is only His face."

From this experience he returns to the dance with the teacher, which is now the dance within his own blood. The teacher tells him, "Next time you will be leading." After the experience of merging we have to live from our own oneness. Once the eye of the heart has been opened, unity leads us to unity. The heart will take us deeper and deeper into states of oneness, allow us to witness Him more and more fully. "In Thy light shall we see light."[18]

At the beginning there is a goal, a path, and a wayfarer. But the experience of union dissolves this illusion. The heart reveals what the mind can hardly grasp. The merging with the teacher continues, but who merges with who? The light within the teacher merges with the light within the disciple, but it is only one light, the "light of the heavens and the earth."[19] "Light rises towards light and light comes down upon light, *and it is light upon light.*" His light illumines Himself, and we are a witness to this unveiling which is both within us and beyond us.

SERVICE AND SEPARATION

Finally the dreamer realizes that "I was only able to have this experience because my feet permanently touched the ground." We need to have our feet on the ground in order to balance the inner experiences of the heart. The demands of everyday life create this balance, without which the heart's opening could easily throw us into psychological and mental instability. Suddenly we are immersed in cosmic oneness and the ego loses its separate identity. Returning to the limitations of ego-consciousness can be painfully disturbing. But we need this limitation in order to balance the heart's expansion.

The Sufi path understands that expansion needs to be followed by contraction: the inner world is balanced by the outer world. The mysteries of the path are contained by ordinary, everyday life. The ego-self can easily become fragmented and unstable after such an opening to the beyond. Living in this world—having a family, a profession, bills to pay, and outer demands to meet—gives the ego a focus and identity after it has been whirled into the abyss of non-being, into the vortex of unity. When you know the heart's freedom, living within the limitations of the outer world may be painful, but it is necessary.

From oneness we return to the duality of everyday life. But because we are separate from Him we are able to serve Him. The knowledge of oneness held in the consciousness of duality is the true profession of servanthood. Separate from Him, we witness that He is One. Without separation there could be no witnessing. There would only be the uncreated oneness. With both feet on the ground we can look up at the heavens and marvel at our Lord; we can look at the creation around us and recognize His hidden face. Within His world of multiplicity we can sing the heart's song that "everything is He."

Ibn 'Arabî writes that "True perfection is found only in the one who witnesses both his Lord and himself."[20] Returning from states of nearness, we witness His oneness and our separation. We witness how the world is a reflection of His unity. Until we have experienced His oneness we cannot fully serve Him because we do not know the true nature of our relationship to Him. Once we have had the experience, we know that only He gives us substance, that He is the center of everything. The dreamer has experienced this, how everything, every atom, every microbe, and every star, is "turning around the center of God," is dancing His song. He returns with this knowledge imprinted into consciousness.

Experiencing the relationship between the creation and the Creator, we come to know the poverty of ourself and all creation. We realize that all our qualities come from Him alone. "O people! You are the poor toward God, and God, He is the Independent, the Praiseworthy!" (Qur'an, 35:15). Poverty and servanthood are bound together: when we realize our true poverty we realize our relationship with God and our position as servant. "None is there in the heavens and the earth that does not come to the All-merciful as a servant" (Qur'an, 19:93). We cannot know God, but we can know our relationship with Him. Through the experience of His unity we come to know our poverty and our servanthood.

Three days after having this experience of the dance of life the friend had another dream:

> I am with my teacher and some other people in a circle. I am allowed to sit next to my teacher since I am new. On the opposite side a dainty little woman with a round-shaped face is sitting. She has glasses on and her eyes are full of light and mercy. I call her "mercyfullness of the heart." I know that this is some kind of conference about the work. I am allowed to be present since I have been "officially accepted" within this circle. And I know that I have to watch first in order to know how the work is done in this group.
>
> When I awoke I thought that this was the circle of *"the servants of humanity."*

"The servants of humanity" are those who have fully embraced the role of servanthood. They belong to the Creator and not to the creation. Obedient to Him, they are free. Knowing unity they have accepted separation, for only within separation can they serve Him in His creation.

Servanthood necessitates our knowing our true relationship with Him. Experiencing that He is the center of everything, we come to know not only our role as servant but also how everything is dependent upon Him. We see the secret structure of the universe and the relationship of the one to the many. Coming back into the world, we bring this knowledge into our daily life, into our role as servant. Passing from separation to unity, we return to separation as the "servants of humanity." The heart's knowledge enables us to work in relationship with the inner structure of all life. We work in harmony with the deepest patterns of life, the dance that is "His song."

BEYOND SILENCE

Silence is the mother of everything that has come out from the Depth. And Silence kept quiet about what she was unable to describe: the Unspeakable.

Clement of Alexandria[1]

NO NEWS RETURNS

Non-being and being, silence and sound, the unmanifest and the manifest, these opposites are the two robes of the mystic, the traveller between the two worlds. Born into creation, we long to return Home, to the Real hidden within the dance of multiplicity. Our longing turns into our spiritual path, attracts us to a teacher, keeps us inwardly focused despite the difficulties of the way. We are ground down and recreated, reborn in a different substance. What we seek we become; we become a part of the infinite emptiness. We are merged within non-being, and yet we remain here, in this world of separation.

The mystic is "a soldier of the two worlds," a traveller who has returned Home and yet remains to tell others of this journey. But what can be said of this journey except that "no news returns"? The moth consumed in the fire of love leaves no traces. The mystic has been made empty, with only a scarred fragment of personality and ego remaining to allow him to live in the world. The real secret, the real meaning is elsewhere, beyond the mind, beyond the known and the unknown:

> The Oneness of God, which is professed by
> the Sufis, consists of: separating the created
> from the non-created, going forth from one's
> native land, rejecting attachments, and putting
> aside what one knows and does not know, so
> that in place of all this there is the Real.[2]

What we seek, what is found, can never be described,
not even known by the mind. Why then speak about
silence or try to create an image of emptiness? Words
are only footprints in the sand that vanish at the water's
edge.

NOTHING CAN BE TOLD OF LOVE

The path to the beyond begins here, in this world. It is
the experience of separation that draws us Home. Only
when we are in a physical body can we reach Reality.
The manifest is an essential part of our journey to the
unmanifest. Only through the limitations of being can
we reach the infinite ocean of non-being. The combi-
nation of the two worlds, of being and non-being,
creates the path. Standing with our feet on the ground
we look to the sky and long for Him whom we love.
Lost for an instant in the ecstasy of His embrace, we
then return to the outer-world of forms, in which His
beauty and His majesty are reflected. The friction of
the inner and outer worlds ignites the flame of passion,
and thus the deepest desire of the soul is born into
consciousness. We do not know for whom we long.
We may call Him Lord or Beloved, but the heart knows
the truth of His unnamable essence.

Rûmî was a lover who knew the limitations of
language:

> I have phrases and whole pages memorized
> but nothing can be told of love.
>
> You must wait until you and I
> are living together.[3]

Words belong to this world, to the manifest, created world in which we are separate, in which we long for His touch. We can only speak of the separation, of the waiting. The experience of the Beloved is always beyond any expression. In the moments of ecstasy all signs are forgotten, all intentions lost.

But without words, how could we proclaim that He is beyond? There is a silence that speaks directly to the heart, that tells of His touch. Yet we are not all heart; we need to drag the rest of ourself to the brink, to include the mind and its need to understand. We need to praise Him even though we *know* our praise is inadequate, that nothing can compare or come close to Him. Through words the mind can come to know that it cannot know, understand that it cannot understand. Then it will give itself more freely to the unknown, lose itself more readily in the silence of love.

My teacher would say about her lecturing that she could just as well say "Baa, baa, baa." She knew the real communion was from heart to heart in the silence of love. But she continued to talk, to try to explain the mysteries of the path, even though she *knew* that she would be misunderstood, that words were so inadequate. When she was with her sheikh in India he explained very little. He would say, "You will know by and by." With her Western mind and its need to understand she found this very difficult, and vowed when she returned to the West that she would try to explain as much as she could. The Western mind is structured differently from the Eastern mind and has been trained and educated in a different way; it "needs to know." The path takes us beyond the mind, which is rightly called "the slayer of the Real," but we cannot just dismiss the mind. The mind has an important function in our daily life and its equilibrium needs to be maintained despite the confusions of the path. When the mind understands, it creates less resistance and surrenders more easily.

Words describe the path and the fluctuations of the wayfarer, the transitions and confusions that we encounter. Sometimes a phrase, a saying of a master, will be a signpost in this unknown land, pushing us deeper into ourself, showing us our own limitations and the pathway beyond. Words help us in the land of separation, in the journey to love's shore. They can carry the energy of one who has passed on, who has separated the real from the unreal. With this energy we are encouraged and given the tools of discrimination to help us make the same distinctions, to know what separates us from our Self.

Turning inward into the heart, we are drawn by the invisible fragrance of love. We follow this fragrance without understanding why. But as we make our journey we catch traces of fellow travellers, of those who have journeyed before us. "We are guided by their footprints" (Qur'an 6:90). The paradoxical words they have left behind begin to make sense and give us encouragement on this most impossible of journeys. For example, when there seems to be no path, we can remember Abû 'Alî ad-Daqqâq's words that "Love is a sweetness, but its inner reality is bewilderment,"[4] and then allow ourself to be lost.

The real loving, the real work on the path, is always within the heart where words can not enter. Words circle around, pointing to this inner chamber, to this place of unveiling. From separation they point towards union. Rûmî writes of words as love letters that "teach beginners about love," no longer needed in the presence of the Beloved:

> When you are mature and with your love,
> the love letters and matchmakers
> seem irritating.
> You might read those letters,
> but only to teach beginners about love. One who sees
> grows silent. When you're with one of those,
> be still and quiet, unless he asks you
> to talk.[5]

Yet Rûmî who was a master of love continued to pour out words, to create a tapestry of love-longing that would inspire millions. Through words he creates an aura in which we can almost taste the mystery he describes. He takes us by the hand and shows us many of the faces of divine love, the laughter, the beauty, and the endless longing. But while he describes his Beloved in so many ways, he knows it is all a way of saying what can never be said, His name:

> Sometimes I call you wine, or cup,
> sunlight ricocheting off those,
> or faintly immersed in silver.
>
> I call you trap and bait,
> and the game I'm after, all
> so as not to say your name.[6]

LOVE HAS NO COLOR

He is one and alone, and there is no comparison. His coloring is love and love has no color. How shall we describe even love? Lovers know that words are too heavy and dense:

> A thing can only be explained by what is more subtle than itself; there is nothing subtler than love, by what then shall love be explained?[7]

In the story of the Kamal Posh, the "blanket wearers," this group of lovers travelled all over the ancient world to every prophet, but no one could satisfy them. One day they came to Mohammed. He just looked at them without speaking, and they were completely satisfied. Why were they completely satisfied? Because he created love in their hearts. The story says that these lovers of God stayed with Mohammed and became the early Sufis.

The silence beyond the mind is the home of love. The heart opens to God and He infuses it with knowledge of Himself, with the textures of loving, the substance of the path. This is the wine "drunk before the creation of the vine," the eternal moment of the soul in which the whole spiritual journey is contained. The circular journey from non-being into being and back to non-being is held in the heart as a promise, and comes into consciousness as longing and the memory of being together with Him. This memory brings the fragrance of loving woven with the threads of silence.

The invisible fragrance that haunts us needs to become a part of our daily consciousness. We are always seeking what we know we cannot find and we need to include this mystery in everyday life, to speak of His lost presence. The repetition of His name, the practice of the *dhikr*, speaks of the potency of words as a way of remembrance. Repeating His name, we reconnect with our lost Beloved. His name gradually pervades our whole being, until every cell of the body knows to whom it belongs. From duality we turn towards oneness as we remember Him. Each time we repeat His name we recognize that we are separate, but this separation cries out with recognition of His eternal presence.

In the ecstasy of oneness there is no name to repeat, no need to remember because nothing is forgotten. But dressed in the cloak of manifestation we carry the mystery of His separation from Himself, and then we need to remember Him. Words help us in this work. He has many names, among which there is His greatest name, *Allâh*, which is always on the lips of many of His lovers. We may also desire to repeat other prayers, for example the powerful protestation of His oneness, "*Lâ ilâha illâ llâh*" (there is no god but God). What we repeat we become. Through His name we return from the manifest to the unmanifest, but we carry the stamp of His majesty, the wonder of His beauty, the knowledge of His oneness.

His Essence cannot be named, nor can it be known. To quote Ibn 'Arabî, "In respect of Itself the Essence has no name...nor is it known by anyone."[8] We come to know Him through His divine names, His qualities as they appear in His creation and are manifest within us. His beauty, His majesty, and His other names appear to us and so we come to know Him. He reveals Himself through His manifestation, through limiting His unknowable Self. On the journey Home we bring this knowledge back to Him; we bring the knowing of His names.

Repeating His name, knowing His attributes, we remember Him. Through our remembrance we incarnate the bond of lover and Beloved, the sigh in the soul. This is a remembrance born within the heart that we bring into the mind. Through our recollection of Him, our repetition of His name, we link together the two worlds, the unmanifest and the manifest. We fulfill our function of lover, to "be here for Him."

Knowing that we are separate, we acknowledge the wonder of separation, the mystery hidden within His names. Standing on the shores of separation, we are not limited to silence, because His creation is full of sounds. We know that all names point to what cannot be named, that they carry this hidden message. The dance of the inner and outer, of being and non-being, is played out in the life of the lover, in the mystery of union and separation.

THE DANCE OF DECEPTION

We are a part of this play of opposites, of this dance of deception that is also a dance of revelation. The whole of creation is a mirror for His face; each atom unknowingly sings His name. The mystic, clearing away the debris of the ego, seeks to *consciously know* what is hidden within the dance. Slowly we polish the mirror within the heart that allows us to see what is hidden. Words may guide us but they belong to this world of duality and can also deceive us. We learn *never to judge by appearances*, for the apparent always hides the real.

Repeating the name of Him who cannot be named,

The Paradoxes of Love

we come close to Him who is both near and immeasurably distant. Surrendering ourself and our own perceptions, we are opened to what remains. My teacher would often purposefully confuse us, watch our reactions and confuse us more. We would believe each word she said and with our belief she would throw us into the abyss. Learning to catch the reflection of what is real amidst the myriad illusions and deceptions of the world is a lifetime's work, and the Sufi group is used as a microcosm for this work. Words deceive, but, charged with the energy of the path, this deception can also be a revelation:

> If one says that He is both the guiding and
>   He who leads astray,
> then all are on the way and no one is erring.[9]

I once had an experience with my teacher in which I was directly confronted by a situation which I knew to be untrue. My teacher firmly denied that something we both knew had actually happened had ever taken place. The power of her insistence together with my respect for her forbade any argument. I had to accept that "black was white." Initially this threw me into a tremendous state of confusion. In any normal conversation or discussion there is an accepted framework of shared belief. For example, if you are talking to someone sitting in a chair, you both accept that the person is actually sitting in a chair. But what happens if the person in the chair absolutely denies that she is sitting in a chair? Then you find yourself in a situation in which there is no mutually accepted framework. This is the situation into which I was thrown. All normal patterns of truth had been demolished by my having to accept that "black was white."

150

What happened was that this experience threw me into my deepest connection with what is beyond duality, my inner relationship with my sheikh, my total belonging to him. When all outer patterns are shown to be deceptive, one can either struggle amidst the destruction, trying to cling onto ruins, or one can leave behind any outer form or identification and turn inward where the only true belonging exists. Sitting in the presence of my teacher I was turned away from the deceptions of the outer world with its limited perception of truth, to an inner reality in which there was only the oneness of absolute belonging. When belonging is total there is only oneness.

This situation brought both confusion and freedom as I was forced to consciously state that I belonged only to my sheikh and that nothing else mattered. I did not mind what happened. I no longer cared if black was white. What appeared a crazy confrontation had thrown me beyond any patterns or identification. The outer teacher had been totally demolished and the inner teacher established beyond the duality of truth or falsehood. I felt like the shepherd whom Moses accused of praying incorrectly. When Moses came to apologize the shepherd only thanked him, for Moses's unjust accusations had thrown him beyond any form:

"You applied the whip and my horse shied and jumped
out of itself. The Divine Nature and my human nature
came together.

Bless your scolding hand and your arm;
I can't say what has happened.

What I'm saying now
is not my real condition. It can't be said."

151

> ...When you eventually see
> through the veils to how things really are,
> you will keep saying again
> and again,
>
> > "This is certainly not like
> we thought it was!"[10]

MASTERS OF DECEPTION

The ego and mind in their normal state are masters of deception. They are forever convincing us of the reality of their limited consciousness, forever telling us that the world is flat. In the arena of the path we are deceived again and again until we learn to use the heart to see what the mind cannot grasp. Through dreams, visions, meditation, intuition, and in my case shock tactics, a different quality of consciousness develops, one that is not bound by appearances or the limitations of reason. We learn to look for the inner meaning, grasp the thread of our own conviction, and watch our own reactions in which the ego's values are most visible.

This inner quality of consciousness is connected to the higher Self and is used to guide us Home. When we turn away from the outer world to seek Truth, we have access to this consciousness, and the more we give ourself to the path the more clearly we can see with its light. Outer confusion combined with a desire for Truth drives us to this higher consciousness which is not caught up in duality. The more we surrender the ego, the more we give up our own patterns of beliefs and habits of mind, the more clearly we are able to see in the light of the Self. Finally we are forced to live in the light of oneness and bring this quality of consciousness into our daily life.

On the outer plane, words are easily caught in contradictions and the interplay of duality. But on the inner plane, words can carry the singleness of Truth. Sentences or phrases that we hear in meditation or spoken in dreams (particularly if they come from an invisible voice) can resonate with this singleness of purpose that does not allow for argument. There is no duality in these phrases for they carry the oneness of the Self.

We slowly learn that if we experience two sides to a situation, we are still imprisoned within the ego—for "where there is a choice there is a lack of understanding." The mystic always looks inward beyond the duality of the outer situation to the core of meaning that carries the white light of the Self. Breaking through the thought-forms of duality requires conviction and power, the inner striving towards oneness, and the belief in this oneness that underlies all duality. Duality carries the comfort of familiarity, oneness the bleakness of the beyond. Even when we have grasped the underlying meaning, the essence of the experience, we need to hold onto it against the attacks of our conditioning and the external world that try to drag us back into the conflicts of duality.

After my experience of having to accept an untruth my mind tried to rationalize the situation. Had my teacher made a mistake? Why did she say such an obvious untruth? But such thoughts only clouded the experience. I knew that I had to stay true to the essence of the experience, a consciousness of oneness that had been imprinted into me. Later I realized the potency of what had happened, the depth of the gift I had been given. I had been made fully aware of an inner connection far stronger than the illusion of right or wrong. Inwardly belonging to my sheikh carries a passion and conviction in which my whole being is surrendered to His will. I was once told in a dream, "One cannot walk the path of straight with rules." The mystic passes beyond the duality of right and wrong into the arms of the Beloved. Belonging to Him is the only support we are allowed.

Bringing the inner oneness of the Self into our daily life is not easy. First we have to listen to its voice, catch the hint. Then we have to live it—live it with conviction and power. Otherwise it is swept aside by the pressures and thought-forms of the outer world. We have to trust, to gamble on our innermost belief and our intuition, which the arguments of the outer world will contradict and try to destroy. Standing up for the Self against the energy of the outer world and the collective requires tremendous determination. At first we are supported in this work by the group and the teacher. They form a "support group" that protects us and affirms the value of our inner belief. But on the path to the Real any outer support is ultimately a limitation. There comes the time when the support of the group will fall away or be broken. Even the outer teacher will turn against us, breaking the container that had protected us, throwing us back upon ourself. When we are so alone, we can either behave like an abandoned child (and these feelings will probably surface), or we can force ourself to trust the One who can never betray us. In Him there is no duality so there can be no betrayer or betrayed. We have to trust both the One and His guidance that comes from within. Faced with the ultimate deceptions of the outer world, we have no alternative.

When we belong to God and look only to Him, all signs point back to Him. He has said, "And we will show them Our signs in the horizons and in themselves" (Qur'ân 41:53). When the eye of the heart is opened, everything is a mirror for His face, everything a sign of His oneness. The lover who has tasted the truth of love knows that He is both the betrayer and the betrayed, both the maker and the dispeller of illusions. Every word has at its core the one word of His name. Every phrase is an act of praise. Beyond duality everything rests in Him, and in the midst of duality there is nothing other than Him:

> "Whose beloved are You?"
> I asked,
> "You who are so
>   unbearably beautiful?"
> "My own," He replied,
>   "for I am one and alone
> love, lover, and beloved
>   mirror, beauty, eye."[11]

THE INNER SILENCE OF THE HEART

The heart has no boundaries because the Beloved has no boundaries. Within the heart there is no place to hide or to be hidden. In the nothingness of meditation, the mind immersed in love has no cares. But when we return to this world, how can we reconcile the insecurity of love and devotion with our individual self and its instinctual need to protect itself? Whose hand is there to guide us, to teach us how to flow between the two worlds? Some mystical paths take their devotees to a cave or ashram, where the outer world hardly touches them. Immersed in inner states, they are protected by their seclusion. But Sufis have always walked a path that takes them into the midst of life:

> One day a man from Mount Locam came to visit Sarî al-Saqatî.
> "Sheikh So-and-So from Mount Locam greets you," he said.
> "He dwells in the mountains," commented Sarî. "So his efforts amount to nothing. A man ought to be able to live in the midst of the market and be so preoccupied with God that not for a single minute is he absent from God."[12]

To the seeker, taking part in life, in the activities of the world, the path reveals His secret face, reveals non-being within being.

Silence is a tremendous protection—not withdrawing in silence but keeping the inner silence of the heart. Talking of daily affairs, we are silent about the real inner states, about the ways of the heart. We keep our inner attention with our Beloved while we engage in the outer activities of life. Enough of the mind is occupied with everyday life to leave us inwardly undisturbed. My teacher could talk for hours about the weather, about the flowers in her garden, while her inner attention was elsewhere. People would sit and listen, not knowing she was not present. Her sheikh would also talk about outer events, the price of butter, trouble on the Indian frontier, yet he was inwardly at prayer or listening to the Beloved.

A Sufi group can embrace the same quality in that while some people talk, others are in meditation. Sometimes one sits in silence while in the distance there is the sound of conversation. Hearing a phrase or two, one returns to meditation. The two worlds blend together, and this develops in daily life. Rather than building a wall of protection, we learn to live in two places at once. At one time I worried that my teacher saw so many people all the time. Then I had a dream in which I saw that her apartment had two floors. On the lower floor there was a large room where she was with many people, but there was also a small upstairs room where she could be alone, undisturbed.

Inwardly we learn to rest in silence. This silence is not the opposite of sound, but underlies sound. Through our meditation and other practices we develop this inner core of stillness that is always with us. The silence which is the heart's home is our own seclusion in the midst of daily activities. Wherever we are, whatever our outer difficulties, turning within we find this inner space, full of silence and peace. Here the two worlds meet and merge together; non-being and being reflect each other. Here we listen to our Beloved, to His words of love and guidance. Contained by silence, His words are protected from the conflicts of the mind. They come from oneness and carry this quality.

As lover and servant we learn to wait in silence, to immerse our inner self in His silence. We try to attune ourself to the currents of love that flow from the inner world. From the inner emptiness where love is born come also words of tenderness and words of guidance. We give Him our utmost inner attention so that He can talk to us and we can catch His hint. He needs us to be attentive to Him. As His words come into consciousness they may become distorted by the mind and personality, but there is always this place within the heart where they remain pure. His servant returns here, to the space of inner communion.

Within the heart there is not the confusion of duality, but a quality of consciousness that belongs to oneness. This higher consciousness of the Self carries the directness of an order and the fineness of His hint. Attuned to the Self, we need to bring this higher consciousness into our everyday mind in order to be guided by His will. In different ways we hear this inner guidance. His hint can come as a prompting, or an idea that surges suddenly from within. Sometimes He speaks to us with a still, clear voice, or a sentence impressed upon our mind. I have learned to be attentive to a thought that comes without any reference to the currrent flow of the mind and its images. In particular, I value a sentence or thought that comes into my mind just as I am coming out of meditation.

We will make mistakes. Many times we will confuse the voice of the ego for the wisdom of His words. We will hear what we want to hear, or distort His guidance with our own conditioning and desires. But His mercy is always greater than His justice and He will help us to return, to reattune our inner and outer self to His way. In humility we stand before Him, knowing our own inadequacy and His greatness. We pray to be of use to Him, the silent prayer of a heart offered up to Him.

Listening within, we need to discriminate between the influences of the mind and ego and what He wants us to hear. This is a discrimination born of love and attention, the devotion that the lover brings to the will of his Beloved. "Thy will be done" is not just a spiritual statement but an attitude of the heart and the mind that look towards God. The work of the lover is to listen to His words and then to bring them into his life. Creating an inner space is the first stage of the work; it is followed by the need to live from this space—to live His will and love in the world.

In our devotion we come to Him. Seeking to be of service, we put ourself in His hands. In the deepest silence of the heart we know that our love for Him is united with His love for us. The circle of love is complete, eternal. This circle has always been there but we have forgotten, or been busy with other things. His greatness is that He cannot betray us, although we can betray Him so many times. He is always listening to us though we forget Him so often.

Finally our heart becomes a mirror for Him, reflecting His love and His will into our life. In our separateness we belong to Him and aspire to live this belonging. But in the depths we *know* that there is no separation, that belonging is born of union. In the depths there is only His unnameable presence, the intoxicating abyss of His non-being. In His kindness to let us come to know Him He created the world, a world in which we can love and serve Him. From being we return to non-being, walking the pathway to the Absolute. Within the heart all the opposites are united. Our tears and our joy trace the circle of our service, as our love and longing draw us to Him.

> Oh Lord, give me a pure heart and an
>   enlightened soul;
> Give me the sigh of evening and the tears
>   of sunrise;
> On the way to Yourself, first make my self
>   without self;
> When I am without self, open the road
>   from Yourself to me.[13]

NOTES

TITLE PAGES, pages i-xii

1. Trans. Oliver Davis, *Beguine Spirituality*, p. 101. The Beguines were a Christian lay movement for women in North-Western Europe that flourished in the twelfth and thirteenth century.

INTRODUCTION, pages xiii-xxvi

1. Quoted by Carol Lee Flinders, *Enduring Grace*, p. 110.
2. Fakhruddîn 'Irâqî, *Divine Flashes*, trans. William Chittick and Peter Lamborn Wilson, p. 120.
3. 'Attâr, *The Book of Secrets*, trans. from the French Lynn Finegan, Chapter V, ll. 548-551
4. 'Attâr, trans. Coleman Barks, *The Hand of Poetry*, p. 59.
5. 'Attâr, trans. Coleman Barks, *The Hand of Poetry*, p. 59.
6. 'Attâr, *The Book of Secrets*, Chapter V, ll. 554-557
7. *Divine Flashes*, p. 105.
8. Quoted by Annemarie Schimmel, *Mystical Dimensions of Islam*, p. 69.
9. Quoted by Schimmel, *Mystical Dimensions of Islam*, p. 63-64.
10. Rûmî, quoted by Chittick, *The Sufi Path of Love*, p. 227.
11. See Sara Sviri, "Between Fear and Hope, On the Coincidence of Opposites in Islamic Mysticism," *Jerusalem Studies for Arabic and Islam*, No. 9, 1987, pp. 321-323.
12. Abdul Latif, quoted by Annemarie Schimmel, *Grace and Pain*, p. 192.
13. Mîr Dard, quoted by Schimmel, *Grace and Pain*, p. 132.
14. Fakhruddîn 'Irâqî, *Divine Flashes*, p. 125.
15. Abdul Latif, quoted by Schimmel, *Grace and Pain*, p. 184.
16. Ibn 'Arabî, quoted by Chittick, *The Sufi Path of Knowledge*, p. 375.

160

SEPARATION & UNION, pages 1-30

1. Quoted by Annemarie Schimmel, *Mystical Dimensions of Islam*, p. 135.
2. Persian Song, quoted by Irina Tweedie, *Daughter of Fire*, p. 87.
3. Quoted by Schimmel, *Mystical Dimensions of Islam*, p. 305.
4. Al-Hallâj, quoted by Louis Massignon, *The Passion of al-Hallâj*, Volume Three, p. 104.
5. Rûmî, trans. Daniel Liebert, *Rumi, Fragments, Ecstasies*, p. 30.
6. Rûmî, quoted by Schimmel, *Mystical Dimensions of Islam*, p. 165.
7. *Hadîth qudsî* (extra-Qur'anic revelation).
8. *Hadîth*, quoted by al-Jîlânî, *The Secret of Secrets*, trans. Tosun Bayrak, p. 15.
9. 'Attâr, *The Conference of the Birds*, trans. C.S. Nott, p. 13.
10. Ibn 'Arabî writes, "The union (*jam'*) which negates all difference while you experience it is not to be counted on; it is ignorance (*jahl*)." Quoted by Muhammad Abdul Haq Ansari, *Sufism and Shari'ah*, p. 39.
11. Fakhruddîn 'Irâqî, *Divine Flashes*, p. 116.
12. Quoted by Schimmel, *As Through a Veil*, p. 32.
13. *Yusuf and Zulaikha*, trans. David Pendlebury, p. 6. See Llewellyn Vaughan-Lee, *The Call and the Echo*, Chapter Five, "The Unattainable Bride," for a detailed discussion of the love affair with the feminine from a mystical perspective.
14. Fakhruddîn 'Irâqî, *Divine Flashes*, p. 85.
15. Qur'an, Sûra 41:53, quoted by Schimmel, *Mystical Dimensions of Islam*, p. 188.
16. "He taught Adam the names," Qur'an, Sûra 2:31.
17. Quoted by Margaret Smith, *Readings from the Mystics of Islam*, p. 36.
18. *Rumi, Fragments, Ecstasies*, trans. Daniel Liebert, p. 16.
19. The *dhikr*, like the *mantra*, is the repetition of a sacred word or phrase, often the *shahâda*, "*Lâ ilâha illâ llâh*" (There is no god but God), or one of the names of God, especially *Allâh*.
20. *Hadîth qudsî* (extra-Qur'anic revelation), quoted by Schimmel, *Mystical Dimensions of Islam*, p. 168.

21. Quoted in *Sufi, A Journal of Sufism*, Issue 24, "A Sufi Calendar of Remembrance."
22. Quoted by Ansari, p. 241.
23. Quoted by Massignon, Volume Three, p. 42.
24. Told by Rûmî, *Mathnawî*, IV, 2138.
25. Quoted by Massignon, Volume One, p. 607.
26. Quoted by Evelyn Underhill, *Mysticism*, p. 436.
27. Bâyezîd Bistâmî, quoted by William Stoddart, *Sufism*, p. 83.

INTIMACY & AWE, pages 31-51

1. Quoted by R.S. Bhatnagar, *Dimensions of Classical Sufi Thought*, p. 89.
2. Bedagi, a member of the Wabankis Nation, quoted by T.C. McLuhan, *Touch the Earth*, P. 22.
3. Because of the nature of these experiences, some mystics (for example Ibn 'Arabî) are often mistakenly labeled pantheists.
4. Quoted by Schimmel, *Deciphering the signs of God*, p. 220.
5. Quoted by Schimmel, *Deciphering the signs of God*, p. 226.
6. Gêsûdarâz, quoted by Schimmel, *As Through a Veil*, p. 67.
7. William Chittick, *The Sufi Path of Knowledge*, P. 23.
8. Sûra 21:23, quoted by Schimmel, *Deciphering the signs of God*, p. 221.
9. Quoted by Schimmel, *Deciphering the signs of God*, p. 222.
10. For a fuller discussion of the surrender to the skeikh, see Vaughan-Lee, *The Call and the Echo*, pp. 130-132.
11. Unpublished quotation.
12. Quoted by Llewellyn Vaughan-Lee, *Travelling the Path of Love,* p. 185.
13. Quoted by Al-Sarrâj, Bhatnagar, p. 137.
14. *Daughter of Fire*, pp.434-435.
15. Tweedie, p. 378. The limitations of everyday life are also good countermeasure to the dangers of inflation. See Llewellyn Vaughan-Lee, *The Bond with the Beloved*, pp. 20-21: "How can you be a spiritually advanced person when

you get angry about a parking ticket? The world continually confronts us with our failings and inadequacies and thus protects us from the dangers of inflation."
  16. Trans. Coleman Barks, *Delicious Laughter*, pp. 30-31.
  17. Chittick, *The Sufi Path of Knowledge*, p. 24.
  18. Quoted by al-Qushayrî, *Principles of Sufism*, p. 27.
  19. 'Attâr, *Muslim Saints and Mystics*, trans. A.J. Arberry, p. 47.
  20. Makkî, quoted by Sara Sviri, "Between Fear and Hope," *Jerusalem Studies for Arabic and Islam*, 9, 1987, p. 332.
  21. Fear is the anticipation of something that might happen, and since the true Sufi is "the child of the moment," "he has no future, therefore he has no fear. In the same manner he has no hope, since hope is the expectation of an agreeable event, or the unlifting up of an unpleasant one." Al-Qushayrî, quoted by Sara Sviri, "Between Fear and Hope," *Jerusalem Studies for Arabic and islam*, p. 345.
  22. Kalâbâdhî, *The Doctrine of the Sufis*, trans. A.J. Arberry, p. 138.
  23. Ibn 'Arabî, quoted by Chittick, *The Sufi Path of Knowledge*, p. 376

LOVE & VIOLATION, pages 52-71

  1. "Mother and Daughter Mysteries," *Woman Earth and Spirit*, pp. 56-7.
  2. Incest symbolically represents the introversion of the energy of consciousness necessary to produce a rebirth of consciousness. See Vaughan-Lee, *The Bond with the Beloved*, pp. 73-74.
  3. Psychic and psychological rape are less understood but can also be very traumatic and wounding. Like incest, rape does not have to be physically enacted, and incest and rape are often related. A mother can have a psychologically incestuous relationship with her son, in which there is no physical abuse, but the son remains a victim, often with his sexuality damaged and the feeling that he has been raped.
  4. Abû'l-'Abbâs al-Karîm, *The Secret of God's Mystical Oneness*, p. 310.
  5. Rûmî, quoted by Schimmel, *Mystical Dimensions of Islam*, p. 191.

6. *Signs of the Unseen,* trans. W. M. Thackston, Jr. pp. 119-20.

7. Rûmî, trans. Coleman Barks, *Say I am You,* pp. 27-28.

8. Bhai Sahib, quoted by Tweedie, p. 469.

9. Abû Sa'îd ibn Abî-l-Khayr, *The Secret of God's Mystical Oneness,* p. 387.

10. *The Conference of the Birds,* trans. C.S. Nott, pp. 102-103.

11. *For Love of the Dark One, Songs of Mirabai,* trans. Andrew Schelling, pp. 107-108.

12. Quoted by William Chittick, *The Sufi Path of Love,* p. 241.

13. Quoted by R.A. Nicholson, *Studies in Islamic Mysticism,* p. 51.

14. *Beguine Spirituality,* ed. Fiona Bowie, p. 81.

15. *Women in Praise of the Sacred,* ed. Jane Hirshfield, p. 115.

THE VEILS OF GOD, pages 72-95

1. Quoted by Chittick, *The Sufi Path of Knowledge,* p. 365.

2. *The Enlightened Heart,* ed. Stephen Mitchell, p. 103.

3. Quoted by Chittick, *The Sufi Path of Knowledge,* p. 401, n. 19.

4. Qur'an, 50:16.

5. 'Attâr, *Muslim Saints and Mystics,* p. 267.

6. The Sufi master Bhai Sahib's final message to Irina Tweedie, *Daughter of Fire,* p. 729. See also Vaughan-Lee, *The Bond with the Beloved,* pp. 118-119.

7. Chittick, *The Sufi Path of Knowledge,* p. 364.

8. *Hadîth,* quoted by Ibn 'Arabî, Chittick, p. 364.

9. 'Attâr, *Muslim Saints and Mystics,* p. 121.

10. *Daughter of Fire,* p. 608.

11. *Daughter of Fire,* p. 498.

12. Quoted by Chittick, *The Sufi Path of Knowledge,* p. 365.

13. Chittick, *The Sufi Path of Knowledge,* p. 45.

14. *Divine Flashes,* trans. Chittick, p. 99.

15. Quoted by Chittick, *The Sufi Path of Knowledge,* p. 43.

16. Ibn 'Arabî, quoted by Chittick, *The Sufi Path of Knowledge,* p. 45.

17. Ibn 'Arabî, quoted by Chittick, *The Sufi Path of Knowledge,* p. 365.

18. Abû Tâlib Makkî, quoted by Ibn 'Arabî, Chittick, *The Sufi Path of Knowledge*, p. 231.
19. *Rumi, Fragments, Ecstasies,* trans. Daniel Liebert, p. 31.
20. *Rumi, Fragments, Ecstasies*, p. 14.
21. 'Attâr, *Sufi Symbolism*, Volume One, Javad Nurbakhsh, p.80..
22. Quoted by Laleh Bakhtiar, *Sufi Expressions of the Mystic Quest*, p. 21.
23. For a description of different types of dreams see Llewellyn Vaughan-Lee, *Sufism, the Transformation of the Heart*, pp. 104-120.
24. Quoted by Louis Massignon, *The Passion of al-Hallâj*, Volume One, p. 614.
25. Henry Corbin, *The Man of Light in Iranian Sufism*, p. 57.
26. Ibn 'Arabî, quoted by Chittick, *The Sufi Path of Knowledge*, p. 329.
27. Only through knowing His Greatest Name, *Allâh*, can we know all of His names, because *Allâh* contains all of the divine names and attributes.
28. Quoted by Schimmel, *Mystical Dimensions of Islam*, p. 272.
29. Jîlî, "The Perfect Man," quoted by R.A. Nicholson, *Studies in Islamic Mysticism,* p. 84.

TWO WINGS TO FLY, pages 96-116

1. *Mathnawî*, II, 1552f, trans. Camille and Kabir Helminski, *Rumi: Daylight*, p. 143.
2. *Mathnawî*, IV, 1357f., quoted by Schimmel, *I am Wind, You are Fire*, p. 71.
3. *Diwân*, "The Soul of the World," trans. R.A. Nicholson, *Rûmî, Poet and Mystic*, pp. 182-183.
4. Quoted by Schimmel, *I am Wind , You are Fire*, p. 71.
5. *Mundaka-Upanishad*, *The Ten Principal Upanishads*, trans. Shree Purohit Swami and W.B. Yeats, p. 56.
6. "Tested by Fire and Spirit," unpublished video interview, 1988.
7. Lao Tsu, *Tao Te Ching*, trans. Stephen Mitchell, 1.
8. Quoted by Bhatnagar, p. 144.
9. Katherine Haynes, *The Cosmic Web*, p. 59.

10. Mahmûd Shabistarî, quoted by Bhatnagar, p. 116.
11. *Fawâ'ih al-jamâl*, trans. by Sara Sviri, "Between Fear and Hope," *Jerusalem Studies for Arabic & Islam*, Vol. 9, 1987, p. 343.
12. Tweedie, p. 226.
13. Tweedie, p. 226.
14. Yahyâ b. Mu'âdh, quoted by al-Qushayrî, *Principles of Sufism*, p. 290.
15. *The Book of Secrets*, Chapter V, ll. 642-3.
16. Trans. N Scott Johnson, "Ocean and Pearls, Ibn Sab'în and the Doctrine of Absolute Unity," *Sufism*, Issue 25, p. 29.
17. Sviri, p. 349.
18. Sviri, p. 344.
19. Kalâbâdhî, quoted by Sviri, p. 346.

OBEDIENCE & FREEDOM, pages 117-141

1. Trans. Coleman Barks and John Moyne, *This Longing*, p. 35.
2. Qur'an, 18: 61-83. See also Vaughan-Lee, *Sufism, the Transformation of the Heart,* pp. 141-147.
3. Quoted by Javad Nurbakhsh, *Sufi Symbolism,* Volume Three, p. 153.
4. Sa'dî, quoted by Javad Nurbakhsh, *Sufi Symbolism,* Volume Three, p. 152.
5. For more detail on the anima within a spiritual context, see Vaughan-Lee, *Sufism, the Transformation of the Heart,* pp. 92-94, and Vaughan-Lee, *The Call and the Echo,* Chapters Four and Five.
6. Quoted by Louis Massignon, *The Passion of al-Hallâj,* Volume One, p. 285.
7. *Confessions,* 8.7.
8. When the eleventh-century Sufi, Abu'l-Hasan Kharaqânî, was asked for the sign of poverty, he replied, "That the heart be black." "Meaning what?" he was questioned. He replied, "No other color exists beyond black." See Vaughan-Lee, *The Bond with the Beloved,* p. 96.
9. Shabistarî , *The Secret Rose Garden ,* p. 30.
10. For a fuller exploration of the theme of spiritual poverty, see Vaughan-Lee, *The Call and the Echo,* Chapter Seven, "The Poverty of the Heart."

11. Lâhîjî , quoted by Henry Corbin, *The Man of Light in Iranian Sufism,* p. 118.
12. 'Attâr, *The Conference of the Birds,* trans. C.S. Nott, p. 124.
13. *Sermon, "Blessed are the Poor." Author's italics.*
14. Quoted by Schimmel, *Mystical Dimensions of Islam,* p. 123.
15. *Hadîth qudsî ,* quoted by Schimmel, *Mystical Dimensions of Islam,* p. 133.
16. Trans. Coleman Barks, "A Basket of Fresh Bread," *This Longing,* p. 70.
17. Trans. Schimmel, *I Am Wind, You Are Fire,* p. 204.
18. Psalm 36:9.
19. Qur'an, 24:35, the "verse of Light." See Vaughan-Lee, *The Call and the Echo,* Chapter Six, "The Relationship with the Teacher."
20. Quoted by Chittick, *Imaginal Worlds,* p. 61.

BEYOND SILENCE, pages 142-159

1. *Excerpts from Theodotus,* 29, trans. by Peter Kingsley, unpublished lecture, 1995.
2. Abû Sa'îd ibn Abî-l-Khayr, *The Secret of God's Mystical Oneness,* p. 55.
3. Trans. Coleman Barks, *Birdsong,* p. 14.
4. Quoted by al-Qushayrî, *Principles of Sufism,* p. 330.
5. Trans. Coleman Barks and John Moyne, *This Longing,* p. 198.
6. Trans. Coleman Barks, *Birdsong,* p. 15.
7. Sumnûn, quoted by Schimmel, *The Mystical Dimensions of Islam,* p. 140.
8. Quoted by Chittick, *The Sufi Path of Knowledge,* p. 62.
9. Dard, quoted by Schimmel, *Pain and Grace,* p. 137.
10. Trans. Coleman Barks and John Moyne, *This Longing,* p. 22.
11. Fakhruddîn 'Irâqî, *Divine Flashes,* p. 111.
12. Vaughan-Lee, *Travelling the Path of Love,* p. 22. Adapted from *The Secret of God's Mystical Oneness,* trans. John O'Kane, p. 379.
13. Persian poem, unknown origin.

BIBLIOGRAPHY

'Abd al-Qâdir al-Jilânî. *The Secret of Secrets*. Trans. Shaykh Tosun Bayrak. Cambridge: The Islamic Texts Society, 1992.

Abû Sa'îd ibn Abî-l-Khayr. *The Secret of God's Mystical Oneness*. Trans. John O'Kane. Costa Mesa, California: Mazda Publishers, 1992.

Al-Qushayri. *Principles of Sufism*. Trans. B.B. Von Schlegell. Berkeley: Mizan Press, 1990.

Ansari, Muhammad Abdul Haq, *Sufism and Shari'ah*. London: The Islamic Foundation, 1986.

Arberry, A.J. *The Doctrine of the Sufis*. Cambridge: Cambridge University Press, 1966.

Attâr, Farîd ud-Dîn. *The Conference of the Birds*. Trans. C.S. Nott. London: Routledge & Kegan Paul, 1961

—. *Muslim Saints and Mystics*. Trans. A.J. Arberry. London: Routledge & Kegan Paul, 1966.

—. *The Book of Secrets*. Trans. Lynn Finegan. Unpublished.

Bakhtiar, Laleh. *Sufi, Expressions of the Mystic Quest*. London: Thames and Hudson, 1976.

Barks, Coleman & Khan, Inayat. *The Hand of Poetry*. New Lebanon: Omega, 1993.

Bhatnagar, R.S. *Dimensions of Classical Sufi Thought*. Delhi: Motilal Banarsidass, 1984.

Bowie, Fiona, ed. *Beguine Spirituality*. New York: Crossroad, 1990.

Chittick, William C. *The Sufi Path of Love*. Albany: State University of New York Press, 1983.

—. *The Sufi Path of Knowledge*. Albany: State University of New York Press, 1989.

Corbin, Henry. *Creative Imagination in the Sufism of Ibn 'Arabî*. Princeton: Princeton University press, 1969.

—. *The Man of Light in Iranian Sufism*. London: Shambala Publications, 1978.

Fakhruddin 'Iraqi, *Divine Flashes*. Trans. Wilson, Peter Lamborn. New York: Paulist Press, 1982.

Flinders, Carol Lee. *Enduring Grace*. San Francisco: HarperSanFrancisco. 1993.

Haynes, Catherine. *The Cosmic Web*. Ithaca: Cornell University, 1984.

Hirshfield, Jane, ed. *Women in Praise of the Sacred*. New York: HarperCollins, 1994.

Jami. *Yusuf and Zulaikha*. Trans. David Pendlebury. London: Octagon Press, 1980.

The Koran. Trans. A.J. Arberry. New York: Macmillan, 1955.

Luke, Helen. *Woman: Earth and Spirit*. New York: Crossroad, 1986.

Massignon, Louis. *The Passion of al-Hallâj*. Princeton: Princeton University Press, 1982.

McLuhan, T.C. *Touch the Earth*. London: Garnstone Press, 1972.

Mirabai. *For Love of the Dark One*. Trans. Andrew Schelling. Boston: Shambhala, 1993.

Mitchell, Stephen, ed. *The Enlightened Heart*. New York: Harper & Row, 1989.

—, trans. *Tao Te Ching*. New York: Harper & Row, 1988.

Nicholson, R.A. *Studies in Islamic Mysticism*. Cambridge: Cambridge University Press, 1921.

Nurbakhsh, Javad. *Sufi Symbolism* Volumes I - IV. London: Khaniqahi-Nimatullahi Publications, 1984-1990.

The Qur'an. Trans. M.H. Shakir. Elmhurst, New York: Tahrike Tarsile Qur'an, 1991.

Rûmî. *Delicious Laughter*. Trans. Coleman Barks. Athens, GA: Maypop Books, 1990.

—. *This Longing*. Trans. Coleman Barks and John Moyne. Putney, VT: Threshold Books, 1988.

—. *Birdsong*. Trans. Coleman Barks. Athens, GA: Maypop Books, 1993.

—. *Say I am You*. Trans. Coleman Barks. Athens, GA: Maypop Books, 1994.

—. *Rumi Daylight*. Trans. Camille and Kabir Helminski. Putney, VT: Threshold Books, 1990.

—. *Rumi: Fragments, Ecstasies*. Trans. Liebert, Daniel. Santa Fe, New Mexico: Source Books, 1981.

—. *Rûmî, Poet and Mystic*. Trans. Nicholson, R.A.. London: George Allen and Unwin, 1950.

—. *Signs of the Unseen*. Trans. Thackston, Jr., W.M.. Putney, Vermont: Threshold, 1994.

Schimmel, Annemarie. *Mystical Dimensions of Islam.* Chapel
Hill: University of North Carolina Press, 1975.
—. *Pain and Grace.* Leiden: E.J. Brill, 1976.
—. *As Through a Veil, Mystical Poetry in Islam.* New York:
Columbia University Press, 1982.
—. *I Am Wind, You Are Fire.* Boston: Shambala Publica-
tions, 1992.
—. *Deciphering the Signs of God.* Albany, New York: State
University of New York Press, 1994.
Scott Johnson, N. "Ocean and Pearls, Ibn Sab'în and the
Doctrine of Absolute Unity, *Sufism,* Issue 25. London:
Kahniqahi Nimatullahi Publications
Shabistarî. *The Secret Rose Garden.* Trans. Florence Lederer.
Grand Rapids: Michigan, 1987.
Smith, Margaret. *Readings from the Mystics of Islam.*
Westport, Connecticut: Pir Publications, 1994.
Sviri, Sara . "Between Fear and Hope, On the Coincidence
of Opposites in Islamic Mysticism," *Jerusalem Studies
for Arabic and Islam,* No. 9, 1987.
Tweedie, Irina. *Daughter of Fire, A Diary of a Spiritual
Training with a Sufi Master.* Nevada City: Blue Dol-
phin Publishing, 1986.
Underhill, Evelyn. *Mysticism.* New York: New American
Library, 1974.
Vaughan-Lee, Llewellyn. *The Lover and the Serpent:
Dreamwork within a Sufi Tradition.* Shaftesbury: Ele-
ment Books, 1989.
—. *The Call and the Echo: Sufi Dreamwork and the Psy-
chology of the Beloved.* Putney, Vermont: Threshold
Books, 1992.
—. *The Bond with the Beloved: The Mystical Relation of the
Lover and the Beloved.* Inverness, California: Golden
Sufi Center, 1993.
—. *In the Company of Friends, Dreamwork in a Sufi
Group.* Inverness, California: Golden Sufi Center,
1994.
—. *Sufism, The Transformation of the Heart.* Inverness,
California: Golden Sufi Center, 1995.
—, ed. *Travelling the Path of Love, Sayings of Sufi Masters.*
Inverness, California: Golden Sufi Center, 1995.
Yeats, W.B., trans. (with Shree Purohit Swami). *The Ten
Principal Upanishads.* London: Faber and Faber, 1937.

INDEX

ACKNOWLEDGMENTS

The author gratefully wishes to acknowledge: for permission to quote from *Beguine Spirituality,* edited by Fiona Bowie, introduction and compilation copyright © Fiona Bowie 1989, translation copyright © Oliver Davies 1989 used with permission from Crossroad Publishing Company, New York; Daniel Liebert, for permission to quote from *Rumi: Fragments, Ecstasies* translated by Daniel Liebert; excerpt as submitted from *Women in Praise of the Sacred* by Jane Hirshfield copyright © 1994 by Jane Hirshfield, reprinted by permission of HarperCollins Publishers, Inc.; excerpt as submitted from *Tao Te Ching* by Stephen Mitchell, translation copyright © 1988 by Stephen Mitchell, reprinted by permission of HarperCollins Publishers, Inc.; Khaniqahi-Nimatullahi Publications, for permission to quote from *Sufi Symbolism* by Dr. Javad Nurbakhsh and from *Sufi,* issue #25, an article titled *Oceans and Pearls, Ibn Sab'in and the Doctrine of Absolute Unity* by Scott Johnson; Maypop Books, for permission to quote from *Delicious Laughter, Say I am You* and *Birdsong,* translated by Coleman Barks; Omega Press, for permission to quote from *The Hand of Poetry* translated by Coleman Barks; reprinted from *Fakhruddin 'Iraqi* by William Chittick and Peter Lamborn Willson © 1982 by the Missionary Society of St. Paul the Apostle in the State of New York.Used by permission of Paulist Press; from *I am Wind, You Are Fire* by Annemarie Schimmel; © 1992. Reprinted by arrangement with Shambhala Publications, Inc., 300 Massachusetts Avenue, Boston, MA 02115; from *For Love of the Dark One* translated by Andrew Schelling, © 1993. Reprinted by arrangement with Shambhala Publications, Inc., 300 Massachusetts Avenue, Boston, MA 02115; reprinted from *Deciphering the Signs of God* by Annemarie Schimmel by permission of the State University of New York Press; reprinted from *The Sufi Path of Knowledge* by William Chittick by permission of the State University of New York Press; for permission to quote from *This Longing* translated by Coleman Barks and John Moynes and *Rumi: Daylight* translated by Camille and Kabir Helminski and *Signs of the Unseen* translated by Thackston Jr. published by Threshold Books, RD4 Box 600, Putney; for the extract taken from *Rumi Poet and Mystic* by R. A. Nicholson, reproduced by kind permission of Unwin Hyman Ltd.

LLEWELLYN VAUGHAN-LEE, Ph.D., has followed the Naqshbandi Sufi Path since he was nineteen. In 1991 he moved from London to northern California, where he now lives with his wife and two children. He lectures throughout the United States and Europe.

THE GOLDEN SUFI CENTER is a California Religious Non-Profit Corporation dedicated to making the teachings of the Naqshbandi Sufi Path available to all seekers. For further information about the activities of the Center and Llewellyn Vaughan-Lee's lectures, write to:

The Golden Sufi Center
P.O. Box 428
Inverness, California 94937

Tel: (415) 663-8773
Fax: (415) 663-9128
e-mail: GoldenSufi@aol.com
website: http://users.aol.com/GoldenSufi/gsc.html

OTHER TITLES PUBLISHED BY
THE GOLDEN SUFI CENTER

BY LLEWELLYN VAUGHAN-LEE

*The Bond with the Beloved:
The Mystical Relationship of the Lover and the Beloved*

*In the Company of Friends:
Dreamwork within a Sufi Group*

*Travelling the Path of Love,
Sayings of Sufi Masters*

Sufism, The Transformation of the Heart

BY IRINA TWEEDIE

*Daughter of Fire:
A Diary of a Training with a Spiritual Master*